PRACTICAL BOATING SKILLS

PRACTICAL BOATING SKILLS

Katie and Gene Hamilton

Illustrations by Christine Erikson

Hearst Marine Books

New York

This book is dedicated to all the boaters who have caught our lines and welcomed us to an unfamiliar harbor, or thrown us a tow line when we needed one. They've made our time on the water the wonderful adventure that it is.

▲ ▲

Library of Congress Cataloging-in-Publication Data

Hamilton, Katie.
    Practical boating skills / Katie and Gene Hamilton; illustrations by
Christine Erikson
        p. cm.
    Includes index.
    ISBN 0-688-13205-7
    1. Boats and boating. I. Hamilton, Gene. II. Title.
GV775.H33 1995
797.1—dc20   94-28750
                                                   CIP

Printed in the United States of America

First Edition

1 2 3 4 5 6 7 8 9 10

BOOK DESIGN BY MICHAEL MENDELSOHN OF MM DESIGN 2000, INC.

CONTENTS

Introduction ix

1 Boat Handling and Helmsmanship 1

2 Getting Under Way 10

3 Docking 14

4 At Anchor 27

5 Trailer Basics 36

6 Waterskiing 42

7 Sailing Basics 45

8 Weather 58

9 Knots 62

10 Laws and Requirements for Safe Boating 66

11 Rules of the Road 80

12 Navigation 86

13 Coastal Piloting 96

14 Electronic Navigation 111

15 Loran-C and GPS 120

16 Cruising 124

Glossary 141

Index 145

PRACTICAL BOATING SKILLS

INTRODUCTION

▲ ▲ ▲ ▲ ▲ ▲ ▲ ▲ ▲ ▲ ▲ ▲   ▲ ▲ ▲ ▲ ▲ ▲ ▲ ▲ ▲ ▲ ▲

Being on the water is better than being anywhere else, and having the practical skills to operate a boat gives you confidence that your time on the water will be enjoyable and safe for you and your passengers. That's what this book is about—learning the skills to enjoy and operate a small boat, whether it's sail or power, slow or fast. Whatever your boating style is, you'll enjoy it more if you have basic boating skills.

Sail and power boats under 30 feet offer the same broad range of enjoyment and adventure as larger boats, but with lower financial and time commitments. The smaller the boat, the less bottom to paint, the less equipment to buy, and the less dockage to pay.

Sailing skiffs and day sailers put you on the water with a minimum of fuss; just push the tiller and hoist sail. Small sailboats can be high-performance boats or stable easygoing craft perfect for one's introduction to sailing. Add a small outboard as auxiliary power and you have a dual-purpose boat.

You'll find a variety of one-design class boats in this category that are popular for racing, since each boat in the class is designed to the same specifications. Many one-design boats are dry-sailed, which means they are stored on land on a trailer. One-design boats are popular for learning to sail, so they're used and raced at yacht clubs and in sailing programs on protected waters. Since all the boats have the same sails and equipment, the skipper's skill is the deciding factor in most races.

As sailboats grow to the 25-to-30-foot range, they can become high-performance racing machines with a wide-open cockpit and small cuddy cabin for stowing sails, or be designed for enjoyable cruising with a comfortable cockpit, plenty of ventilation, and accommodations below deck. Sailboats with a center cockpit offer two separate cabins. Some are designed with a large cockpit for sailors who spend most of their time aboard under sail, while others feature creature comforts like a dinette and navigation station rivaling those of much larger boats. Boats in this size with swing keels can be trailered.

Sail-furling systems allow sails to be rolled up like window shades, making sailing easier. Lazy jacks are devices to keep the mainsail under control and on the boom as it is lowered. These are both nice features, especially for a cruising couple or a boat with limited crew members.

The smallest powerboats are personal watercraft, the one-, two-, and three-person boats resembling a snowmobile that you sit or stand on to operate. The jet boat, a relatively new category in the 14-foot range, is designed to carry four passengers, go fast, jump waves, and tow water-skiers. A runabout usually seats four people, often with additional seating forward through a walk-through windshield. Outfitted with a camper pop-top, they can be used for boat camping and overnight cruises.

Center-console boats have plenty of walkaround space, making them a good choice for fishing. Sport boats and cruisers are similar in design, with a V-berth cabin forward, and can be trailered to boat ramps. As powerboats get larger, their hull and power plant determine their speed; layout varies depending on whether they are designed as performance boats or express or sedan cruisers. Still in the under-30-foot category are tugboat designs and trawler-type powerboats, which cruise at lower speeds. They have seaworthy hulls and are less costly to operate because of their fuel-efficient engines. Another type of powerboat is the shallow-draft houseboat with a pontoon hull and spacious trailerlike cabin. Powered by one or two outboards, such a houseboat is well suited to protected waters and river cruising. A smaller version of a houseboat is the platform or pontoon boat, which is ideal for inland lakes. Some of them now feature built-in seating, coolers, and an enclosed head.

Visible on waterways today is a reminder of boating in days past—restored wooden boats. These lovingly refurbished vintage boats are popular with boat clubs throughout the country, which hold regattas and rendezvous where the boats are a featured attraction.

BUILDING BOATING SKILLS

Before you jump aboard, slip the lines, and cast off, review the basics of piloting skills and navigating techniques to operate a boat safely and confidently. These apply to all recreational boaters, whether they're going out for an afternoon of waterskiing on an inland lake or sailing along the coast on an extended cruise. With these skills learned and practiced, you'll enjoy years of boating on whatever type of boat you choose.

The first several chapters of this book deal with seamanship skills and the basics of handling a sailboat or powerboat in a variety of situations. You'll learn the importance of knowing a few basic knots and tricks for tending dock lines that will secure your boat safely in a slip. For safety's sake, you'll find everything you need to know to equip and operate your boat so it meets all U. S. Coast Guard requirements.

Later chapters go into the details of navigating inland lakes and rivers as well as coastline waters. The U.S. Inland Rules of navigation are discussed, with illustrations to show you how to maneuver your boat in various situations when you encounter other boaters. Channel buoys, daymarks, and lights are explained so that you will be well prepared to interpret what they mean. The basics of piloting are discussed so that you will know how to use nautical charts and navigational equipment and determine where you are on the water in relation to land. You'll learn how to calculate distances while going from one destination to another and how the weather, tide, and currents are all factors in safe boating.

Planning a cruise is an important part of a vacation cruise, and it can be almost as much fun as the actual adventure. In the last chapter you'll find advice about choosing a destination to match your cruising style and how to make sure you leave your home port with the right provisions, spare parts, and cruising accessories. It includes plenty of how-to advice about boat camping, anchoring out, and marina-hopping, everything from roughing it in the great outdoors to cruising with all the comforts of home.

Let's go boating!

BOAT HANDLING AND HELMSMANSHIP

odern powerboats and sailboats under power are so reliable and easy to handle that they can often be driven like an automobile. But unlike autos, boats travel on a fluid highway. The most inexperienced skipper can steer a boat in a straight line on a calm day, but mix in a little wind or current and even a basic maneuver can be challenging.

Just as boating can be tricky at times, it is also rewarding. There is always something to learn or a new skill to develop. Volumes are written on fishing, sailing, navigation, but in all these works there is a core of basic information that is not difficult to understand or put into action. This section lays out the basic information and skills that will give you the confidence to operate your boat safety under power. Of course, no one can become an "old salt" just by reading this book. The information is here, but it's up to you to put it to use.

Steering a boat under power is not too much different from driving a car. Turn the helm to the right and the bow of the boat begins to move to the right; turn the helm to the left and the bow moves to the left. That's where the similarity ends. Besides the obvious difference between the water that a boat travels through and the solid ground that a car rolls on, there are fundamental differences in the way a car and boat respond when you turn the wheel or helm.

Sailboats and powerboats under 30 feet offer features and accommodations to suit the needs of boaters whether for an afternoon on the water or an extended cruise.

BASIC TERMS

Boats not only respond differently from cars, they don't even turn right or left—they turn to starboard or port. Boats don't back up, they make sternway, and boats going forward through the water are making headway.

This can get a little confusing at first, but to talk about boat handling it's necessary to understand these four fundamental terms. Since you may face forward or backward depending on which way you are steering the boat, it's not clear to talk about going to the right or left—right or left can be different depending on which way you're facing.

To clear up this potential language problem, boaters refer to the left and right side of a boat as port and starboard. Port and starboard always refer to the left and right side of a boat while facing its bow. A boat turning right is going to starboard; a boat is "turning to port" when it is moving to the left as you face the bow.

While backing up or making sternway, your boat is "going to starboard" if the stern is moving to starboard even though the stern is going left from your point of view while you face backward. Remember, there is only one port or starboard side of a boat, and it's defined while facing forward.

This may be difficult to remember, because the lingo may be new to you, so here's one way to remember which direction is port and which starboard:

A boat is said to be turning to port when the bow is swinging to the left. When making sternway, a boat turns to port when the stern moves to port.

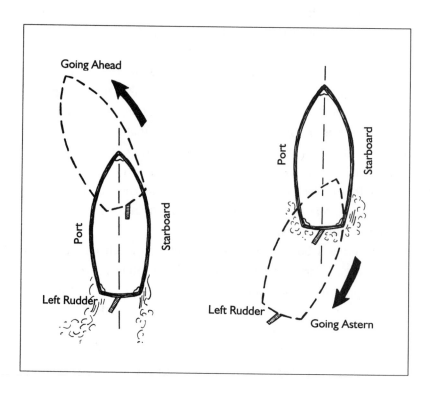

Port wine is red, and so is the blood in your heart, which is on your left side. Also, the port side of a boat has the red running light. If you're right-handed, think of yourself as being "starboard-handed."

Once you can get these basic terms down, most nautical babble will begin to make sense.

When you turn the steering wheel or helm of a boat, you turn the rudder, stern drive, or outboard. It does not matter what moves when you turn the helm—you are considered to be turning the rudder. If you give your boat right rudder, it will turn to the right or starboard; left rudder, and it goes left to port. The same is true for backing up. If you give it right rudder, the stern will go to starboard (even though you may be facing backward and the stern moves to your left), and left rudder causes the stern to swing to port.

Boats travel through the water, which can itself be moving. A boat is said to be making headway when it is moving forward through the water and sternway when going in reverse or backing up. Since the water may be moving, your boat could be going through the water but not moving over the bottom. For example, if you are idling along at, let's say, 1 knot, and the current facing your boat is moving in the opposite direction at 1 knot, you are making headway through the water. But if you look over to the shore or a nearby dock it will appear that you are standing still. This is an important fact to consider when maneuvering a boat through current. Just remember that a boat's movement through the water may not directly correspond to its movement over the bottom.

SHIFT AND THROTTLE CONTROLS

Except for the most basic small outboard engine, most boat engines are controlled by throttle and shift levers. These controls are connected to the engine by cables, or on some larger boats, by hydraulic lines.

The throttle controls the speed of the engine. Pushing it forward increases speed, pulling it back reduces speed, and pulling it all the way back slows the engine to idle.

Most outboard and stern-drive boats have a single-lever control that functions as both shift lever and throttle. When it is in the center position, the engine is at idle and the transmission is in neutral. Pushing the lever forward shifts the transmission into forward. From that point on, pushing the lever forward increases the engine speed. Of course, the opposite is true. Pulling the lever backward puts the transmission in reverse, and further backward movement increases the engine speed.

Boats with separate shift and throttle levers operate in basically the same way as the single-lever types, but there are two separate controls for throttle and transmission. Neutral is found in the center position, usually with the handle standing straight up. To put the transmission into forward gear, push the shift lever forward; to reverse, pull the lever back. Marine transmissions should be shifted from forward to reverse only when the engine is at idle or running very slowly.

All movement of the shift and throttle should be done smoothly and deliberately. Alert everyone aboard that you are about to get under way, and then push the shift lever forward to put the transmission into forward gear. Advance the throttle only after you hear or feel the transmission shift into gear. If you are in congested waters, continue at idle speed until you are out in the clear away from other boat traffic. Remember to watch your wake—you are responsible for your boat's wake and any damage it may cause. Good seamanship and common sense dictate consideration of others.

Before you shift the transmission into reverse, pull the throttle lever to idle. If the engine was running fast, allow a second or two for it to wind down before you shift from forward into reverse or from reverse into forward. One of the advantages of a single-lever throttle and shift control is that the engine is automatically slowed as you pull the lever back to shift the transmission into reverse.

STEERING WITH A WHEEL

Unlike most cars, which steer with the front wheels, a boat is controlled by turning the rudder, stern drive, or outboard motor at its rear. You turn the steering wheel or helm to starboard and the steering gear turns the rudder, stern drive, or outboard motor to starboard, applying right rudder. This pushes the stern of the boat to port and swings the bow to starboard, and the boat begins to turn.

Turn the wheel to port and the opposite happens; the stern swings starboard, turning the bow to port. The rudder, stern drive, or outboard motor can't turn the boat unless the stern is free to swing in the opposite direction. This is important to remember when maneuvering near a dock or another boat, because if you turn the wheel too sharply the stern of the boat may swing over and hit the dock or the other boat.

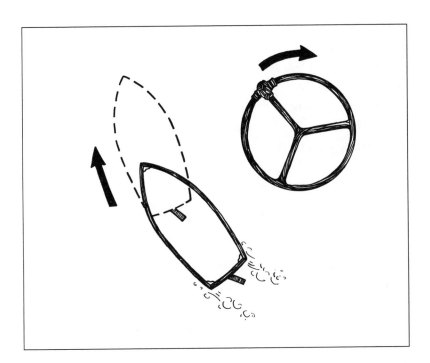

As you turn the steering wheel to the right, the rudder, stern drive, or outboard swings to the right and applies right rudder. This moves the stern to port and the bow to starboard.

STEERING WITH A TILLER

Steering a boat with a tiller or outboard motor that has a tiller arm is different from steering with a wheel, because you move the tiller in the direction opposite from the direction you want to turn. Moving the tiller toward the starboard side of the boat causes the rudder or outboard to apply left rudder, pushing the stern to starboard and turning the boat to port.

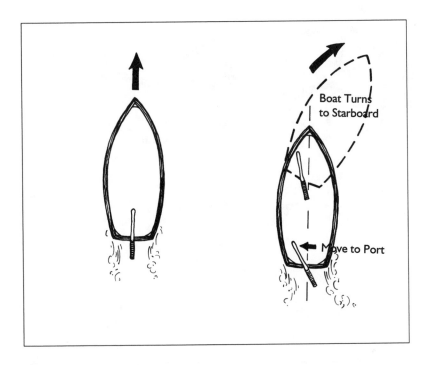

To turn a boat with a tiller, move it in the direction opposite to the direction you want to go. Push it to port and the boat will turn to starboard.

It does not matter which side of the tiller you are sitting on—just remember to move the tiller away from the direction you want the bow to go. If you are steering a sailboat, it is best to sit on the high side of the boat when it heels over in a breeze, to help keep the boat level. Being in this position also gives you the best grip on the tiller. Of course, when the boat changes tacks you have to move to the opposite side of the boat.

GOING STRAIGHT

Steering a boat with either a wheel or a tiller comes naturally to some, but has to be practiced by most of us. Fast, lightweight planing-type boats are very responsive to the helm. When on plane they respond instantly to even a slight turn of the steering wheel or movement of the outboard's tiller. Steering this type of boat is more like driving a car. As soon as the wheel is moved, the boat begins to turn, and it stops turning as soon as the wheel is centered.

Heavier, slower displacement-type boats are slower to respond to the helm. There is a slight lag between the time the steering wheel is turned and the time the boat actually begins to turn.

Each type of boat responds a little differently to the helm. And even identical boats respond differently depending whether they are fully loaded or empty. Wind and wave conditions also affect how a

Oversteering a boat is a common problem until you get used to how your boat reacts to the helm. Use slow, deliberate helm movements instead of fast, sharp ones when steering.

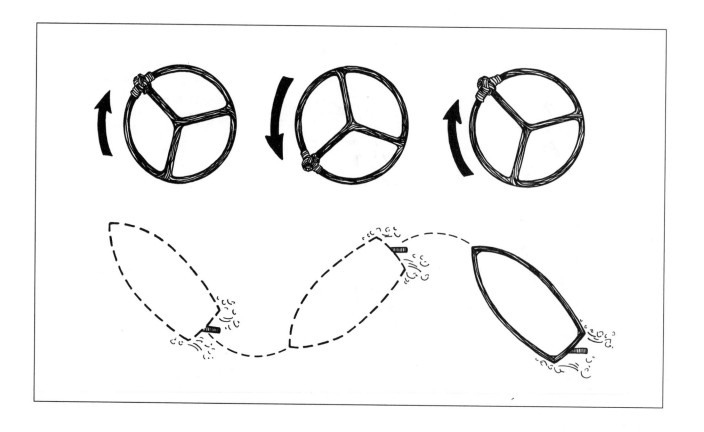

boat steers. There is no substitute for experience, so the more you operate your boat in a variety of conditions, the better helmsperson you will become.

Most inexperienced skippers oversteer or turn the helm too much at first, because there is a natural tendency to turn the wheel until the boat begins to respond or turn. Because of the slight delay between turning the steering wheel and the boat's turning, the wheel is usually turned too far. The boat then starts to turn a little quicker than expected and the wheel is turned the other way until the boat begins to straighten out. Again there is a delay, so the wheel is turned too far and the cycle is repeated. The tendency to oversteer is greatest when going slow, because the boat takes longer to respond to the helm.

You can check yourself out on a calm day. Under power, steer a straight course for several minutes, and then look back at your wake. If it's forming a shallow S, then you are oversteering. If so, let go of the wheel or tiller and allow the boat to steer itself for a couple of seconds. It will eventually wander to the right or left. When it does, turn the helm a tiny bit in the opposite direction and hold it there. If the boat does not respond in five to ten seconds, then turn the wheel a bit more. Eventually the boat will begin to straighten out, and if you have been patient enough, it will not start to swing into a turn in the other direction, but continue straight. The sign of a good helmsperson is keeping a boat on course with the least amount of helm movement.

TURNING

Turning the rudder of a boat causes it to move right or left, which makes the water push harder against one side of the rudder than the other. This uneven pressure moves the rudder to one side or the other, and since it is attached to the boat it moves the stern of the boat with it.

For example, when you give a boat a little right rudder, the rudder moves to the starboard, causing the passing water to push on the starboard side of the rudder. This pushes the stern of the boat to the left or port, causing a turn to starboard. The key phrase here is "passing water." If there is no water flowing past the rudder, there is no force generated. Your boat must be moving through the water, or at least water must be moved past the rudder, for the rudder to turn the boat.

Most rudders are positioned behind the propeller and thus can help turn a boat even when it's not moving. If your boat is shifted into forward, the turning propeller will push water past the rudder

▲ ▲ ▲
HOW TO TURN A BOAT WITHIN ITS OWN LENGTH

Propeller torque, which tends to make backing up a challenge, can be used to good advantage in a tight maneuvering situation. By using short bursts of forward and reverse you can turn a boat in its own length. With a right-hand propeller, turn to starboard, and with a left-hand propeller, turn to port.

Slow down and put the helm all the way over to starboard. When you're halfway through the turn, shift into reverse and the propeller torque will push the stern to port as you stop. Then shift into forward and give a short burst of power, and as soon as the boat begins to move forward, shift into reverse. Continue until you complete the turn.

▼ ▼ ▼

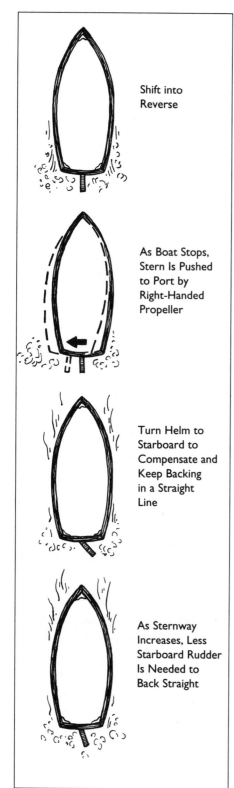

Shift into Reverse

As Boat Stops, Stern Is Pushed to Port by Right-Handed Propeller

Turn Helm to Starboard to Compensate and Keep Backing in a Straight Line

As Sternway Increases, Less Starboard Rudder Is Needed to Back Straight

To back up, shift into reverse and, as the boat stops, turn the helm to starboard to compensate for the tendency of the stern to move to port. As you gain sternway, most boats require less starboard rudder to back up in a straight line.

and so the rudder will turn the boat even though the boat has not yet started to move through the water. This fact comes in handy when you are maneuvering your boat in tight quarters.

Stern-drive or outboard-powered boats can also be turned while standing still, since the propeller is turned with the stern drive or outboard. The water discharged from the turning propeller forces the stern right or left, even though the boat is not moving through the water.

Don't forget that your boat can't turn if its stern is not free to swing in the opposite direction. If you are next to a dock or other obstruction, pull away from it at a shallow angle. Turning the rudder too sharply will cause the stern of your boat to swing into the object.

If you are towing another boat and secure the towline to a stern cleat on one side of the boat, you may have trouble turning the boat, since the heavy pull of the towline restricts the movement of the stern. That is why professional ski boats tow water-skiers from a tow bar located in the center of the boat, which allows the stern to swing freely while turning.

The same principles apply when turning as when steering a straight course. To avoid oversteering while turning, take into consideration the lag time between helm movement and when the boat actually begins to turn. When you're running fast, the lag is usually short; it gets longer as you slow down.

The best way to learn how a boat responds to the helm is to practice steering under various conditions. Make approaches to docks and other objects at slow speed and note how long it takes for your boat to respond to the helm.

In most cases, it is easier to maneuver a boat at slow speeds if you anticipate the turn and begin it a few seconds before you actually want the boat to begin its turn. This is better than putting the rudder all the way over to get the boat to respond quickly. When you turn the rudder sharply in the opposite direction it causes back-and-forth oscillation, which you want to avoid.

STOPPING AND BACKING

Since a powerboat doesn't have brakes, you shift into reverse gear to stop it. However, shifting into reverse is not as sure a way to stop as applying the brakes of a car. Shifting into reverse only works at slow speeds, because unless it is a jet-drive boat, throwing it into reverse at high speeds will usually destroy the transmission, something you want to avoid.

Shifting into reverse gear causes a few easily overcome handling problems. When you shift into reverse, the propeller begins to push water under the boat and away from the rudder. And unless water is flowing past the rudder, it can't turn the boat.

Inboard boats respond very poorly to the helm while stopping, but usually regain steerage as soon as they begin to back up and make sternway. Depending on which way the propeller rotates, it moves the stern to port or starboard while backing down. Once your boat is stopped in the water the prop wash will begin to flow past the rudder and you will regain steerage.

As the boat picks up speed the rudder becomes effective, but if it's a single-screw boat, backing up can be a frustrating experience. Depending on the shape of the hull and the direction the propeller turns, single-screw inboard boats have a tendency to back to port or starboard as soon as you shift into reverse. You can use this to your advantage in some docking situations. But the only way for you to get most inboard boats to back up in a straight line is to turn the helm in the opposite direction so that the rudder overcomes the turning force of the propeller.

Most single-screw inboard boats have right-handed propellers—that is, they turn clockwise when in forward—so they will tend to back to port (counterclockwise) when shifted into reverse. If your boat has a left-handed prop, then expect it to back to starboard when you put it into reverse.

When you shift a right-handed propeller into reverse, it will tend to push the stern to port as you begin to back up. If you apply some right rudder most boats can be made to back in a straight line. You will have to experiment to learn how much right rudder is needed. Generally, more reverse rudder is required when your boat begins to move backward and less as it gathers sternway. With a right-handed propeller you may have to use full left rudder to get your boat to turn to starboard when backing, and you may even find out that she will not back to starboard at all. Hands-on experience is the only way to discover the handling characteristics of your boat.

Outboard, stern-drives, and jet-drive boats are not as much of a problem, since they don't rely on rudder action to maintain control. Since the propeller is turned when the helm is moved, the discharge current from the propeller or jet drive turns the boat. Boats with these power systems tend to stop in a straight line and back straighter than single-screw inboards.

GETTING UNDER WAY

 ost skippers and crew are anxious to get under way, especially when it's a hot sunny day. Here are several things to check before heading for open water.

AT THE DOCK

Unless you have a small sailboat without an engine or an outboard, your first concern is to ventilate the engine compartment to remove any explosive fuel vapors that may have accumulated during layup. All boats with inboard or enclosed engines must have a blower system to ventilate the engine compartment. Make it a habit that the blower switch is the first switch to be turned on when you set foot aboard.

Stow all gear, food, coolers, and clothes carefully. Don't leave items lying around loose in a boat, because they can be blown or dropped overboard easily. When you bring guests aboard, review with them the location of safety equipment and how to use it. You don't have to give a lecture; just make sure everyone knows where safety equipment is located and how to use it. This includes fire extinguishers, life jackets, and distress signals. Ask all aboard, especially children, to put on their PFDs (personal flotation devices) before getting under way.

Get a current local weather forecast by listening to the marine weather on a radio, or check with other boaters for a current forecast.

Before starting the engine, check the fuel level, and if it's an inboard or stern-drive engine, check the oil in the crankcase. Carry enough fuel so there's a reserve amount. Figure you'll need a third of the total for going out and cruising and another third to return, and have at least a third as a reserve supply. This may take a little calculation on your part, but it will prevent anxiety later as the fuel gauge approaches the "E" and you still don't have your home port in sight. A change in weather can force you to change your destination plans, so don't leave the dock without more than enough fuel.

DEPARTING

Pulling away from a dock can be uneventful or full of adventure. Basically the maneuver to leave a dock is just to untie the lines and pull away. Sometimes there is a little more to it than that. Some preplanning before slipping any lines goes a long way to assure a smooth departure.

Unplug and disconnect any power cords, water hoses, or other support lines and stow them away.

Observe what the wind and current are doing. Look at mooring lines and note which are under strain to tell which way the boat will move when you cast off. Another trick is to loosen your line and observe which way your boat begins to drift. If it moves away from the dock, then you can untie the boat and allow it to drift away from the dock before you get under way. If it is held against the dock by wind, current, or tide, then you know you are going to have to do some maneuvering before you can pull away free.

If there's no current, tide, or wind to contend with, release the boat from the slip by loosening the lines. If you leave the lines in the slip or attached to pilings, coil them loosely and stow them on a chock or on top of the piling so they will be easy to retrieve when you return. Don't let them fall into the water, because a loose line can get caught in a prop, not to mention become slimy from marine growth in the water.

If you take mooring lines with you, undo them from the dock one at a time, holding the boat off when it is floating free. With several crew members aboard, this can be done simultaneously. With limited crew, release lines working from the bow backward.

▲ ▲ ▲

TAKING ON FUEL

When you are at the fuel dock, turn off the engine, turn off all radios and instruments, and instruct those aboard who are smoking to put out cigarettes. Turn the bilge blower or exhaust fan that removes fumes from the engine compartment on. Check to see if you smell gas fumes before accepting the fuel hose from the dock attendant. When you receive the hose, hold the nozzle in an upright position so no fuel drips on the deck.

Fill the tank at a rate that will not cause an overflow, and don't leave the fuel running into your boat unattended. When you are finished taking on fuel, replace the fill pipe cap and then return the hose to the attendant. Check the bilge for gas and fumes before you start your motor.

If you have an outboard motor with a portable tank, disconnect the hose from the outboard to the tank and carry the tank to the gas dock to fill it.

▼ ▼ ▼

The stern of a boat swings in the opposite direction to the turn, so pull away from a dock at a shallow angle to avoid banging the stern into the dock.

When pulling away from the dock, remember that your boat steers from the rear and its stern will swing toward the dock as soon as you turn the helm away from the dock. Before putting the gear into forward, give the bow a push away from the dock, and pull away at a shallow angle to avoid banging the stern quarter of the boat into the dock.

USING SPRING LINES

If you are moored between other boats, you can't pull away from the dock at a shallow angle. Wind and tide may also be holding you against the dock. Faced with this situation, experienced skippers of larger yachts rely on their mooring lines to get them out of tight spots. Here's how you can do it.

Most boats use four lines. The bow line runs from the bow cleat on the boat to a post or cleat on the dock. The stern line is usually led from the outboard corner of the stern to a cleat or post on the dock. The forward spring line runs from the bow back to a cleat or post on the dock located close to the center of the boat,

Back slowly against an after spring line to move the bow away from the dock. This will allow you to pull away from a dock where you are sandwiched between two other boats.

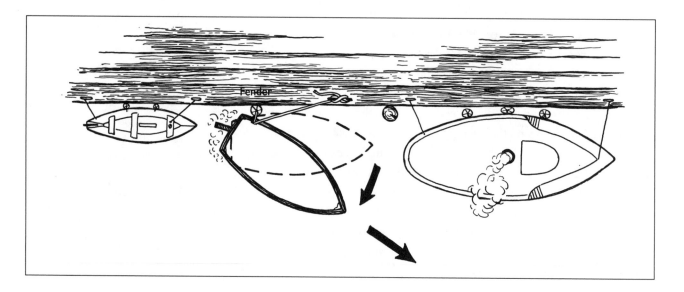

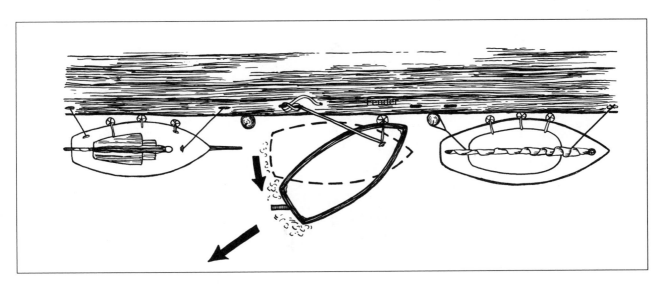

and the after spring line runs from a cleat on the inboard stern to the same cleat or post on the dock.

Most of the time the bow of your boat can be pushed away from the dock with a good shove so you can pull away at a sharp enough angle to avoid the boat ahead of you and avoid banging the stern into the dock. However, when wind or current are pushing the boat against the dock, a good shove is not enough.

In this case, notice which way the current or wind is pushing your boat. If you leave the dock heading into the wind or current, you will be able to maintain maximum control at low speed. If your boat moves forward against her lines, then it's best to back away from the dock. If the boat is pulling back on the lines, pull away going forward. In either case, a spring line can be used to help get the boat turned away from the dock.

To pull away forward, rig an after spring line from the dockside stern cleat to a post or cleat on the dock. Loop the line over the post or cleat and run it back to your boat so you can cast it off from the boat. Then cast off all lines, give the bow a push, and put the boat in reverse with left rudder. Then shift into forward and turn the rudder toward starboard. Be sure the spring line is tight enough so you can't back into the boat behind you. The boat will move backward a foot or so and come tight against the spring line. It will then begin to pivot about the spring line as the bow moves away from the dock. You may have to place a fender between the dock and the corner of the stern to protect it from the dock or piling. As soon as the bow is far enough out to clear the boat ahead, center the helm and shift into forward and proceed out. As you pull out, have a crew member release the after spring line by pulling on one end until it's retrieved on board.

If you want to back out of a tight area, use a forward spring line. In this case, you need to protect the bow of the boat from the dock or piling with a fender.

Move ahead against a forward spring line to swing the stern of your boat away from the dock. This will allow you to back away from a dock where you are sandwiched between two other boats.

DOCKING

N o matter what size boat you have, sooner or later you will have to approach a dock or slip and tie her up. Of course, this does not have to be a traumatic experience, because with a little practice, you can maneuver in and around docks and in close quarters like an old salt.

MOORING LINES

Like other parts of your boat, lines have names and they perform specific functions. For most boats under 30 feet, the four basic mooring lines are all you need. As a general rule, your bow, stern, and forward and after spring lines should be at least as long as your boat and have an eye splice at one end. Nylon braid or laid line is the preferred material.

On boats under 20 feet, it is probably best to secure the end of a mooring line to the cleat on your boat and adjust the line from the dock. On larger boats where it is easier to walk on the foredeck to tend the line, it is better to secure the end of the line to the dock and adjust the line at cleats on board. This allows you to adjust the lines without having to get off your boat, which is more convenient if you have to make a line adjustment late at night.

▲ ▲ ▲

SQUELCHING SQUEAKY DOCK LINES

To get that annoying squeak out of dock lines rubbing in a chock or around a cleat, soak them in a solution of half water and half liquid fabric softener for two or three hours. Let them dry, and the next time you use them, you'll notice there's no squeak.

▼ ▼ ▼

Before beginning an approach to a dock or slip, decide whether you want the looped end of lines going ashore to be secured to the dock or secured around the deck cleat on board. To secure the line to the cleat, wrap the end of the line around the base of the cleat one full turn and then bring the line up over the cleat, crossing over its top and under the other horn. Pull the line up over the other side of the horn, leading it over the top of the cleat and under the other horn to form a figure 8. Before you pull the line tight, put the end under the crossing line to form a half hitch. Give a tug on the end of the line to snug everything up. Placing more turns on the cleat will not increase its holding power, it will just take you longer to cast off the line.

Bow and stern lines are used to hold a boat parallel to the dock. The bow line leads from a cleat on the bow of a boat to a post or cleat on the dock. The stern line leads from a cleat on the

Most small boats can be safely moored to a dock with bow and stern lines and forward and after spring lines.

Stern Line

Bow Line

To secure a line to a cleat, wrap the end around the base one full turn and bring it up over one horn of the cleat and under the other, making a figure 8.

stern of a boat to a post or cleat on the dock. At times, especially in tidal waters, you will find it's better to lead the stern line from the outboard stern cleat of your boat to the dock, because it forms a longer run and a better angle off the boat.

Spring lines prevent a boat from moving forward or aft. The forward spring line prevents the boat from moving forward and is led from a cleat on the bow back to a post or cleat on the dock located about midship of the boat. The after spring line keeps the boat from moving backward and leads from the stern cleats to the same cleat that the forward spring is secured to. If there is no cleat or post amidships, lead these lines to the cleats or posts that the bow and stern lines are secured to. (That's why it is a good idea to have lines at least as long as your boat.)

If a boat has a cleat located amidships, rig both forward and after spring lines from it forward and aft to the same dockside cleats or posts that the bow and stern lines are secured to.

Under calm conditions with no wind and current, you can tie up to a dock with just a bow and stern line. Secure the bow and stern lines to dock cleats or posts well ahead and astern of the boat so they can also function as spring lines.

If there is current, rig a spring line against it. For example, if the current is coming at the boat, rig an after spring line to prevent the boat from going backward. You don't need the forward spring unless the current, wind, or other conditions change. This arrangement holds the boat parallel to the dock under the prevailing conditions. Since conditions can change, don't leave a boat moored this way unattended.

In tidal waters, where a boat moves up and down with the rise and fall of the tide, be sure to lead lines from the boat to the dock at an angle. You might find it's better to lead the stern line from the outboard stern cleat to the dock so there's a longer run between the boat and dock. This is also true for spring lines. If your boating waters have a tide of several feet, you may want to secure long spring lines to posts or cleats closer to the bow or stern instead of amidships.

MOORING TO A DOCK

The key to maneuvering around docks is to go slowly but keep enough headway to maintain steerage. Many lightweight boats with large stern-drive motors idle along pretty fast, but don't steer well unless they are in gear. If you have a boat like this, you can maintain good control at slow speeds by shifting into neutral and allowing the boat to coast, then shifting into gear while turning. Working the shift lever this way allows you to go slow and maintain good control.

In a boat with a right-handed propeller, your easiest approach to a dock is a port-side landing. Before you begin an approach, have fenders rigged and bow and stern lines ready. Approach the dock at about a 30-degree angle. When you get close to the dock, give your boat right rudder to start it turning parallel to the dock.

When the boat is a few feet from the dock, shift into reverse. The propeller will help pull the stern toward the dock as it stops the boat. You may have to apply some left rudder to move the stern if you have an outboard, stern-drive, or jet-drive boat.

When the boat has stopped, secure the bow line and then the stern line. Then secure the spring lines, if necessary. If you use the

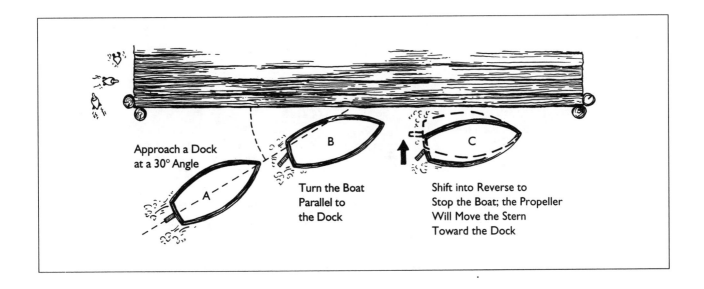

Approach a Dock at a 30° Angle

Turn the Boat Parallel to the Dock

Shift into Reverse to Stop the Boat; the Propeller Will Move the Stern Toward the Dock

propeller action to help move the stern toward the dock you will be surprised at how short a space you can work your boat into.

If you are short-handed or if there is an offshore wind that wants to blow the boat away from the dock, rig a forward spring line. Secure it to a midship cleat, if possible. Approach the dock in the same way, only pass the spring line ashore to be secured first. Then give the boat right rudder and put it into forward. It will move ahead on the spring line and pull itself snug against the dock and stay there as long as you allow it to idle in forward. You then have plenty of time to secure the bow and stern lines without having to worry about the bow or stern blowing away from the dock. This approach is especially useful for larger powerboats and sailboats with limited crews.

A starboard-side approach is no different if you have an outboard, stern-drive, or jet-drive boat, but the propeller action of a single-screw inboard with a right-hand propeller can create some perplexing problems. As soon as you shift into reverse, the propeller will begin to move the stern to port away from the dock. The best way to overcome this is to approach as slowly as possible while still maintaining steerage. Put the helm over to the left to bring the boat parallel to the dock and leave it there as you shift into reverse. As the boat stops, the stern may swing away from the dock slightly. If this happens, shift into forward for a short burst, and the propeller will send a quick shot of water against the rudder and push the stern toward the dock. Shift quickly back into neutral before the boat has a chance to gain headway.

Whenever you approach a dock, always consider the effect that wind and current will have on your boat. Water is much denser than air, so usually a little current will affect a boat more than a lot of wind, especially if it is a sailboat with a deep keel. But if the boat has a fly bridge or tall fishing tower, the wind may be the controlling factor.

Determine whether the current or wind affects your boat the most. One method is to stop dead in the water and observe which

Use a forward spring line to dock if you're short of crew or if there's a strong offshore wind. Secure the forward spring line ashore first, then give the boat right rudder, put it in forward, and allow the engine to idle. The boat will stay against the dock as long as the engine is in gear.

way the boat moves. If the wind and current are opposed, does it move in the direction of the wind or current? If the wind is at right angles to the current, then note how fast it is drifting downwind.

If possible, always approach the dock so that you are heading into the current, because the speed of the oncoming current will slow you down in relation to the stationary dock. For example, if you approach a dock into a $1/2$-knot current running parallel to it, you still are traveling $1/2$ knot through the water when you are stopped in relation to the dock. This is a great help, since you can approach a bit faster and maintain steerage the whole time.

The opposite is true if you approach down-current. In this situation you have to stop the boat and get it going $1/2$ knot backward before you are stopped at the dock. Reversing has to be strong enough to stop the boat and start it making sternway.

SLIPS

You may keep your boat moored in a slip or as a visiting boat be assigned one when visiting a marina or yacht club. The main difference between tying a boat in a slip and tying a boat at a dock is that the boat is secured on both sides in a slip instead of on one side alongside a dock. Boat slips are formed by a combination of short finger piers and pilings. The bow and stern of a boat are tied to the pilings so the boat floats free, secured without contact with the pier.

When approaching a slip, first decide which side of the slip you want to tie up to, and forget about the other lines until that's accomplished. Usually one side of the slip has a finger pier or some way to get off your boat. For example, let's say the dockmaster assigned you to a slip for an overnight stay and the finger pier is on the port side.

Before you enter the slip, secure fenders on the port side so you can come into the slip and pull over to that side without worrying about dinging up your topsides. Rig bow and stern lines on both port and starboard sides, securing the lines to the deck cleats. Be sure to lead these lines under the lifelines so they can run free to the dock. Rig lines on the starboard side so they're ready, but you only have to be concerned with securing port-side lines when you enter the slip.

If you have crew aboard, instruct one to man the port bow line and another to man the port stern line. Station the crew with the stern line about amidships so he can place a looped line over the outer piling as you enter the slip. Proceed into the slip as far as possible and have the crew with the bow line step off the boat

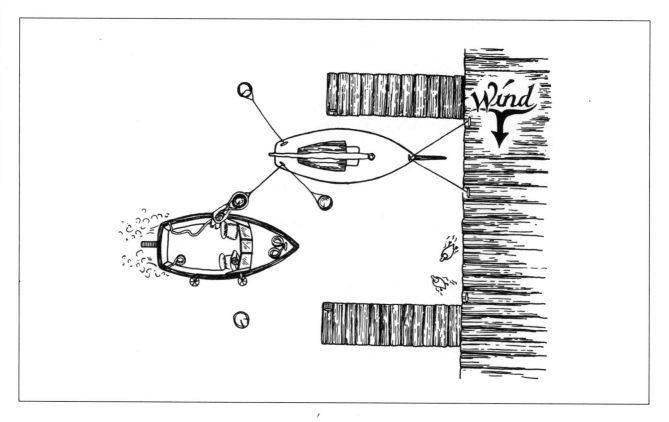

If you're pulling into a finger slip in windy conditions, favor the upwind side. Put a crew member amidships to place a line on the upwind stern piling as you enter the slip. Check the height of the dock before you approach so you can position the fenders correctly between the dock and the topsides of your boat.

and secure the line to a cleat on the finger pier, usually at the front port side of the slip. If there is no cleat, he should secure a line around a piling at the bow of the boat. At the same time, the crew with the stern line can take up the slack so the stern line will not allow the boat to hit the front of the slip. Then he should go forward and toss the starboard bow line to the dockside crew, who should secure the line to a piling or cleat. To get an aft line to the starboard piling, you have a few choices: lasso the piling with a line; wrap the line around the hook on a boat hook and push the line around the piling; or loosen the three other lines and push the boat off the rear port-side piling so the boat drifts over to the starboard piling so you can put the loop over it. Then cleat the line down on deck.

In windy conditions or if there is a crosscurrent, place the stern line on the upwind or up-current piling first so the boat can drift down on the finger pier and you can get the bow lines ashore. If the finger pier is upwind or up-current, favor that side of the slip when you enter and have the bow crewman step off quickly before you begin to drift away.

When bow and stern lines are secure, adjust them at the cleats on deck so the boat rides in the slip without hitting the pilings or finger pier. Depending on the size of your boat and the slip, this may not be possible if there is a large tidal range in your area. If that's the case you may have to rig fenders along the sides to protect the boat.

PICKING UP A MOORING

In most parts of the country, moorings are used for both temporary and permanent anchoring. A mooring is a permanent float or buoy anchored in the water with a line that's sometimes marked with a flag pennant so you can find it. Often the line is left to float free. When you pick up a mooring, remember to approach it from down-wind or down-current, whichever has the most effect on your boat. To find out, observe boats that are moored nearby to see which lie downwind or down-current from their moorings. Choose a boat that is similar in size to yours, because boats of different sizes and shapes are affected differently by the wind and current.

Sometimes you have to supply your own mooring line and pendant; other times there's a short piece of line with an eye spliced in its end already attached to the float. This makes picking up the mooring easier, but take a good look at the line before you haul it aboard—it may be slimy and full of marine growth if the mooring is not used very often. If that's the case, rig your own line.

Have a crewman on the bow with a boat hook and a line with an eye splice ready. Secure the end of the line with the eye splice to a cleat so the other end can be led through the shackle or ring on the top of the mooring buoy. Since the mooring buoy will most likely be obscured by the bow of your boat, communicate with your crew with hand signals. The same hand signals described in the anchoring section work just fine in this situation.

As the boat approaches the mooring buoy, shift into neutral, and then into reverse to stop near the buoy. Have the bow crew snag the shackle or ring on the top of the buoy with the boat hook and pull the mooring to the boat. Slip the line through the ring and

Approach a mooring from downwind. Station a crew member on the bow with a boat hook and a line ready to pass through the ring on the mooring buoy.

lead the end back to a bow cleat and secure it. Make sure the other end of the line is also still secured to the boat before you begin to drift backward and the dock line comes under strain.

Pay out (release) enough line so the boat is far enough from the mooring buoy not to bump into it with the wave action. Unless you have a very long line, you usually can't let out too much line. Look at the other boats—if you let out too much line in a crowded mooring area you risk bumping into other boats when the wind goes calm.

Leaving a mooring is basically the reverse of picking one up. Make sure that the bow crew releases the plain end of the line so it runs freely through the shackle or ring on the mooring buoy. If you let go of the end with the eye splice by mistake, it will get jammed in the shackle and you will have to retrieve it with the boat hook and then release the other end. Before you release the mooring line, decide just how far back you can go before you get tangled up with another boat. In a crowded mooring area you may have to release the mooring line, back up a bit, and then put the helm over and go forward to pass on the downwind side of your mooring. Also look ahead to determine the best way to thread your way through other moored boats to the open water.

BOAT HANDLING IN LOCKS

The vast river and canal system of the United States provides some of the best cruising grounds in the country. This system was a key to the economic development of the country, and today many of the major river systems are navigable through a series of dams that maintain the water level at predictable depths. At each dam there is a lock that allows commercial and pleasure craft to pass up and down stream.

A lock is a large compartment with watertight doors at each end. The water level inside the lock is adjusted to match that of the river so that boats can move from one dammed-up river section to another. The fact that water seeks its own level allows a lock to function without any pumps. In most locks the water level is controlled by large valves. If water from the upriver side of the dam is allowed to flow into the lock, the water level inside the lock will rise until the water in the lock is at the same level as the upriver water. If the water is allowed to flow out of the lock, it will empty until the water in the lock is level with the downriver water.

A typical locking-through cycle goes something like this. If a boat is traveling downriver, the lock is flooded until the water level in it is the same as upriver. The upriver gates are opened and the boat enters and ties up inside the lock along the lock walls. The lock doors or gates are closed and the water drains out of the lock. When the water level inside the lock has matched the downriver level, the downriver gate is opened and the boat unties from the wall and proceeds out of the lock. Then upbound boats enter the lock and the process is reversed.

Going through a lock successfully depends on knowing what to expect and how to maneuver your boat. On most river systems, pleasure boats are allowed in the lock chambers along with commercial vessels, unless they are carrying flammable cargoes like petroleum products. Sometimes small pleasure boats are instructed by the lockmaster to tie alongside these vessels. A small boat may be told to tie onto a large pleasure boat also locking through. This makes it easy, because the larger vessel is against the lock wall cushioning the turbulence as the water flows into or out of the lock chamber.

PREPARATION

If you go through locks on a regular basis or are going through a long series of locks, designate special lines, fenders, and fender boards for this purpose. Most locks have dirty, rough walls that will chew up fenders. The best solution is to make two fender boards from 2 × 6 wooden planks. Hang the fender boards in front of the fenders so that the wood rubs against the lock wall and the fenders cushion the board against the hull. Be mindful of the fender boards when you are locking up. Keep an eye on the boards to be sure they don't hang up on a rough area of the wall as the boat rises.

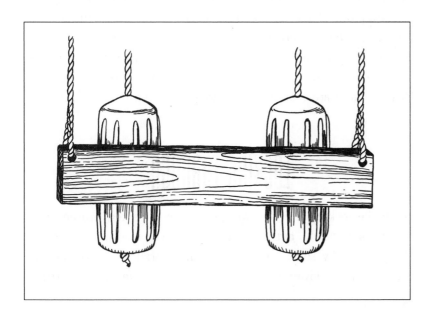

Use 2 × 6 wooden planks as fender boards in front of fenders so that the wood, not the fenders, rubs against the rough lock walls.

Depending on the size of your boat and the configuration of the lock, you may need a couple of very long lines. Some locks have movable bollards that are recessed in the wall and that you tie a line to. Other systems provide bollards along the deck of the lock, so bow and stern lines should be long enough to run from the boat up around the bollard and back to the boat. These lines should be long enough to cover twice the distance from the bottom of the deepest lock you plan to traverse, so that you can control them from the boat, letting out or taking up slack as needed.

SIGNALS

Since the lock and dam systems throughout the United States have been developed over a long period of time, each system has a different, though very similar, system of signals. Each major river or canal system publishes locking information. For example, New York State, which administers several canal systems, including the Erie Canal, publishes maps and locking instructions. The Corps of Engineers provides similar information for the systems it manages on the major river systems.

Locking procedures vary, but all systems require you to approach the lock with caution and wait for a signal from the lockmaster before entering the lock chamber. A red light indicates that the lock is in use, so stop or don't proceed.

Some systems also have a yellow signal, but all systems display a green light when it is safe to enter the lock chamber. Horn blasts are also used to signal when to enter. Generally, it is obvious that you can't enter the lock when its gates are closed, and you have to wait for all the boats in the lock to exit before you can proceed in.

Stay out of the path of the boats coming out of the lock. If you are on the downriver side of a lock waiting to lock up, don't get too close to the lock, because as the water empties from the lock chamber above you'll experience turbulence close to the lock. Most of these areas are clearly marked, so heed the warnings.

LOCKING THROUGH

When the lockmaster gives you permission to enter, proceed into the chamber slowly, but with enough headway to maintain control. There is usually some turbulence at the entrance to the lock, especially on the downriver side. Inside the lock the water is usually

calm. Move directly to a mooring station as directed by the lock-master.

Small boats can usually tie up to one of the ladders provided along the sides or walls of the lock chamber. Usually bow and stern lines can be looped through the ladder rungs to hold the boat in position. As the water level changes, the lines can be moved up or down the ladder.

If you are instructed to tie to the outside of a larger boat, approach it after it is secured in the lock. Approach the boat with your crew holding a bow and stern line for its crew, and offer to come aboard to help tend lines and fend off. The advantage is yours, because your boat will ride up or down without touching the slimy lock walls and your fenders won't be chewed up.

Be prepared to tend lines as your boat moves up or down with the water level in the lock. Secure only one end of the line to your boat and have someone tend the other end. Don't secure both ends of the line to a cleat. Loop the line under the horn of the cleat and make a single crisscross over the cleat so you can pay out the line or pull it in while the cleat takes most of the strain.

Have plenty of fenders ready, as boats are usually rafted together inside locks. On some river systems, like the Illinois River, recreation and commercial boats lock through together.

Locking down is generally a smoother ride than up because the water is draining out of the lock. If you are locking up, the water in the lock will become turbulent as it flows into the lock. On some lock systems the lock door is opened slightly to allow some water in. If this is the case, be prepared for a current running toward the back of the lock at first, followed by a current in the opposite direction. The water sloshes around in the lock until it has filled.

When the water level in the lock is equal to the river or canal, the gates are opened. Don't rush to untie until the lockmaster gives the signal to exit the lock. Give boats ahead of you plenty of room to navigate before you start out. Sometimes large commercial tugs will leave first, and they can create a very turbulent prop wash.

If you are one of the first boats to exit, expect some turbulence at the lock gates, because the movement of the large doors through the water usually causes whirlpools and small eddies at the mouth of the lock. Keep a firm grip on the helm and proceed with enough power to maintain control.

AT ANCHOR

Anchoring a boat overnight in a quiet cove is a popular choice for a cruising boater. Some other reasons you might have to anchor are to give you time to inspect a problem with the engine or sail rig and to find a safe haven from open waters when a squall hits.

Here's a rundown of how to anchor so you're ready and able when the time comes to drop the hook.

GROUND TACKLE

A quick trip down the aisles of a marine supply store and you will find an amazing assortment of anchor types and sizes. Basically all these anchors can be divided into two categories: anchors that get their holding power from their weight, like the mushroom anchor, and those that bury themselves in the bottom, like the Danforth and plow.

Except for the very small sizes used by small fishing boats, mushroom anchors are usually used for permanent moorings. Burying-type anchors provide the most holding power relative to weight and are used by most boaters today.

There are several manufacturers that produce patented anchor designs, and each manufacturer conducts tests to determine the holding power of its anchors. From this data it publishes recommendations about the size of anchor needed to hold boats of different sizes. In general, these recommendations are overkill for occasional anchoring in protected water, but they are too conservative if you expect to ride out a major storm at anchor.

Small lightweight boats under 15 feet should have at least a 5/16-inch-diameter nylon anchor line and 10 feet of 3/16-inch chain. For short stops to anchor while fishing, a mushroom anchor is a good choice. Mushroom anchors are also available with flukes that dig into the bottom and increase holding power. The folding grapnel anchor is also a good choice for fishing.

Neither of these anchors should be used for overnight or unattended anchoring. For more secure anchoring, choose at least a 4-pound aluminum version of the lightweight Danforth type. This style of anchor is available in steel or aluminum and is generally referred to as a Danforth type even though Danforth is a particular brand name. There are several manufacturers of these anchors, which provide high holding power for their weight and are suited for use on small boats.

Larger boats up to about 25 feet should use 150 feet of 3/8-inch nylon line connected to at least 15 feet of 1/4-inch chain. This short section of chain adds considerably to the holding power of any anchor. The weight of the chain helps hold the anchor line close to the bottom so it exerts an even pull parallel to the bottom.

The three most popular and useful anchor styles for pleasure boats are the Danforth, the plow, and the mushroom.

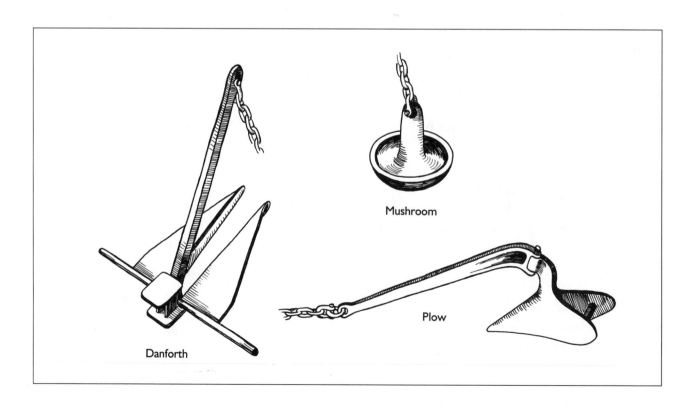

Mushroom

Plow

Danforth

Consider this the minimum amount of chain. If you are going to rely on your anchor in all conditions, increase the chain length; most authorities recommend a section of chain at least as long as your boat.

Lightweight aluminum anchors provide great holding power for their weight. In ideal conditions a 5-pound anchor will have no problem holding your boat, and it makes a good lunch hook when you want to drop the anchor for a short time. If your boating plans will take you away from local waters into areas where you may have to rely on your anchor in all conditions, consider having a primary anchor in the 12-to-25-pound range, in addition to the lunch hook. In poor holding conditions or during a storm, an anchor must have a certain amount of mass to penetrate sea grass and hard bottoms. The larger anchor is also much stronger, since it is heavy enough to have thick shanks and strong flukes.

Boats in the 26-to-30 foot range need strong ground tackle to anchor safely. Use at least 200 feet of $1/2$-inch nylon line attached to 25 feet of 3/8-inch chain. This line and chain attached to at least a 15-to-35-pound anchor should form your primary anchoring system.

In addition to the primary anchor, you should have a second anchor and anchor line and chain. Many boats carry a lighter secondary anchor for use as a lunch hook. Any of the lightweight-type anchors of about 7 to 10 pounds will serve this purpose. Most experienced cruising skippers have two primary anchor sets backed up by a lunch hook. You will find with two reliable anchors you can safely secure your boat.

The size and type of ground tackle should be governed by the type of boating you do. For the weekend boater who cruises close to home port and plans to overnight at marinas, a single lightweight anchor will do just fine. If you have more ambitious cruising plans and choose to anchor overnight in a variety of places, then you need at least two complete sets of ground tackle, which includes anchor, line, and chain.

CHOOSING A SAFE ANCHORAGE

There are many factors that make an anchorage safe. First of all, an anchorage should provide protection from waves and wind. Such protection is usually found in the lee of the land. The ideal anchorage provides protection from all directions and sometimes is called a hurricane hole, but such anchorages are not easy to find. Depending on where you are boating, you may have to settle for an anchorage behind a sandbar that provides protection from the waves, but not wind. Or you may find yourself anchored behind an island that provides shelter from the prevailing wind, but not from waves, which curl around the island and create an uncomfortable roll in the anchorage.

Needless to say, the anchorage must be deep enough to float your boat in all conditions, but yet not so deep that you have a difficult time securing the anchor. Choose an anchorage with water deep enough at low tide to provide at least 3 or 4 feet under your keel.

Nautical charts have depths adjusted to mean low water or the average low tide. Wind and barometric pressure can produce water depths that are much lower than charted. At different times of the month, the moon and other heavenly bodies affect the tides, resulting in lower than charted depths. Consider all of these factors when choosing an anchorage.

Bow Cove is a good anchorage because it has good protection from the weather and is deep enough to allow a couple of feet of water under the boat at low tide, but not so deep as to make anchoring difficult.

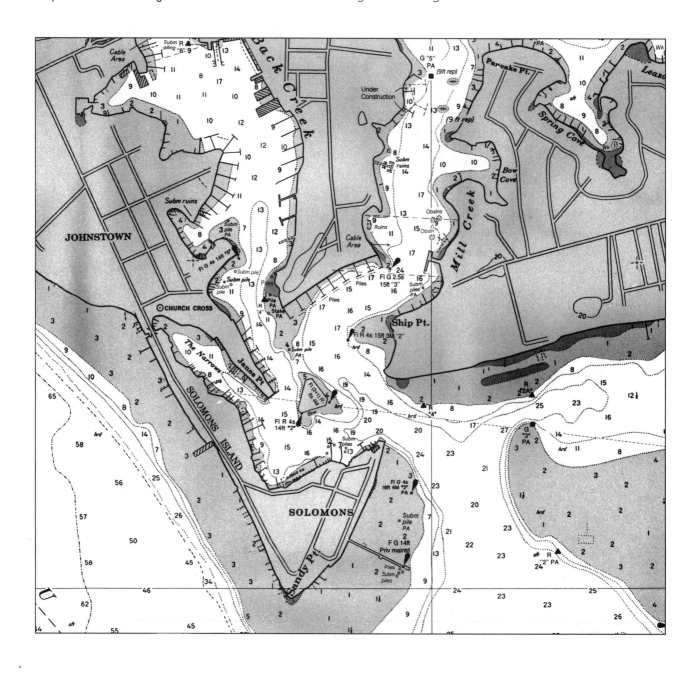

In addition to water depth, a nautical chart has bottom conditions printed on it. The best holding will be found in areas with sand, mud, or clay bottoms. Rocky areas should be avoided if at all possible. Most soft bottoms are suitable, but if the bottom is very soft, your anchor may drag during high winds. You can test the holding power of the bottom by backing down against the anchor with your motor in reverse. If you can drag the anchor through the muck, find another spot.

The deeper the water, the more anchor line must be let out and the larger the radius your boat will swing when there is a change in wind or tide. To anchor safely in 15 feet of water you have to let out over 100 feet of anchor line. Since your boat can swing in a 360-degree circle, you need a clear area around your anchor of at least 200 feet in diameter. The deeper the water, the larger the circle. Always take the swing of your boat into consideration when choosing an anchorage.

ANCHORING TECHNIQUES

Anchoring is not difficult even in adverse conditions if skipper and crew prepare for the procedure. Most of the problems inexperienced skippers face are caused by lack of planning. What you want to avoid doing is to charge into a crowded anchorage, throw a large wake, and then toss an anchor off the bow in a tangled mess of lines. That's an anchoring disaster waiting to happen.

Instead, get the ground tackle on deck. If the anchor is not made up and stored on deck, get it out and attach it to the anchor rode or chain. Double-check that the shackle is tight and that the chain and some rope are flaked or folded on deck so the anchor can be lowered easily into the water without fouling.

Proceed slowly into the anchorage and choose a spot to anchor. If there are already boats lying at anchor, circle the area, noticing how boats are riding at their anchors. Approach the drop point, slow the boat, and then shift into reverse gear to stop. Then signal the crewman on the bow to lower the anchor. Instead of shouting directions between helmsman and crew, use hand signals to communicate. Hollering into the wind is difficult and disturbing to everyone who has to listen; the sound of voices carries on the water.

Slowly and gently lower the anchor into the water until it rests on the bottom. Don't throw the anchor into the water, because it may become tangled in the line as it sinks to the bottom. By the time the anchor reaches the bottom, the boat will probably begin to drift backward with tide or current. In calm conditions, shift into

▲ ▲ ▲
MARKERS IN THE ANCHOR LINE

For a few dollars you can buy a set of fluorescent plastic markers that tell you how many feet of anchor line you have payed out. These handy tabs are set into the anchor line by separating the line and then pulling them through the strands. To install them you need a long stretch of dock or floor space and some sort of marking system like a yardstick so you space them accurately.

When you are anchoring, the markers appear in the line, and you know exactly how many feet of line you have payed out.

▼ ▼ ▼

Above: Before lowering the anchor into the water, check that the ground tackle is ready. This includes attaching the anchor to the chain or rode and seeing that the anchor line is free of tangles.

Above right: To communicate when anchoring, use hand signals instead of shouting.

reverse and back down; as the boat gathers sternway, shift into neutral.

Let out anchor line as the boat backs away from the anchor and pull the line so it remains straight and can't get tangled. Let out line about five times the depth of the water. For example, if it's 10 feet depth, let out about 50 feet of anchor line. Snub the line around a deck cleat. Let the line come tight to set the anchor, and then release more line until it's about seven times the water depth. When the line comes tight again, put the engine in reverse and back down against the anchor.

If the anchor line becomes tight and remains that way, the anchor is holding. If it wavers between tight and loose, the anchor is probably dragging. Decrease the engine power and the anchor will probably reset itself.

When the anchor appears to be holding, look toward the shore and align a tree or other object with something behind it or on the horizon. If the relationship between the two objects does not appear to move, you can be certain the anchor is holding. If the anchor is dragging, you will probably have to pull it up and reanchor at another location with better holding ground.

Scope = L/D

When the anchor line is secured on deck and the engine is shut down, look around the anchorage to notice your relationship with the surrounding boats and landmarks. Take a few bearings of objects on shore and write them in a log so later you can check your position against the bearings to make sure the anchor is holding. If possible, choose lighted objects so you can use them at night.

Good anchoring etiquette dictates this procedure:
- Approach the area where you want to drop the anchor from downwind or down-current.
- Drop anchor behind another boat and then drop back away from it as you let out anchor line.
- Don't "anchor on" or ahead of a boat and then drop back toward it. That puts your boat over the other boat's anchor, which its crew will have difficulty retrieving.

In some anchorages where there is a tidal current change or where space is restricted, lying at a single anchor allows too much freedom for a boat to swing. When the tide changes and a boat swings 180 degrees to face a new current, a single anchor may not reset itself. In this situation, use two anchors in what is commonly called a Bahamian moor. This technique limits the swing of a boat and assures that one anchor is always set facing the current.

Note that even though the anchors are set opposite each other, with one astern of the boat, both anchor lines are secured to the bow so the boat can swing freely into the current. This is not the same as anchoring with a stern anchor attached to the stern. An anchor line attached to the stern prevents the boat from swinging

The correct amount of anchor line in an anchorage is determined by the depth of the water. Let out enough "scope" or anchor line so there's seven times the water depth. In windy conditions, let out more line.

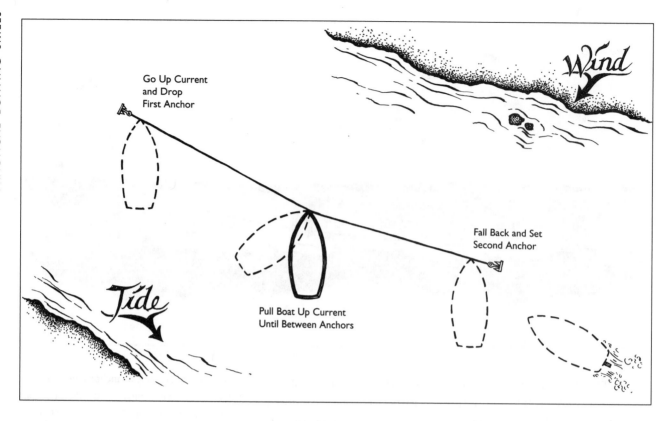

Go Up Current
and Drop
First Anchor

Wind

Fall Back and Set
Second Anchor

Tide

Pull Boat Up Current
Until Between Anchors

A Bahamian moor uses two anchors set from the bow to limit the swing of a boat. With two anchors set, you don't have to rely on a single anchor resetting itself when the wind or tide changes.

to face the changing current or wind. If either is strong and your boat gets broadside to it, chances are that both the bow and stern anchor will drag.

The easiest method to set two anchors in a Bahamian moor is to set the first anchor up-current or upwind, whichever is stronger, just as you would for a single anchor. Then after it is set, let out twice the anchor line necessary and lower the second anchor into the water. Then pull the boat back toward the first anchor with the first anchor line while you let out the other anchor line. When you are between the anchors, give a good pull on the second anchor to set it.

WEIGHING ANCHOR AND WHAT TO DO IF IT'S STUCK

Getting an anchor up is basically the reverse of setting it. Unless there is a strong current running or the wind is blowing hard, you can usually pull the boat up to its anchor by hand. If the strain on the anchor line is heavy, put the boat in forward gear and motor up to the anchor. Do this slowly so the person on the bow can gather in the anchor line and keep it from getting under the boat and fouling in the propeller. Using hand signals, the bow crewman tells the helmsman which way to steer to get over the anchor, since the angle of the anchor line leading to the anchor usually can't be seen from the helm.

When you're pulling the anchor line by hand or motoring up to the anchor, the boat will have some headway as it gets over the anchor. This momentum can be used to help break out the anchor. As the anchor line gets short and leads straight down to the anchor, snub the line on a cleat and allow the boat's momentum to break out the anchor. The bow person should signal when the anchor is free from the bottom.

When the anchor is free, put the engine in forward and proceed slowly until the bow person has the anchor cleaned off and out of the water. If you go too fast the anchor will be pulled under the boat and bang against the topsides when it is hoisted aboard. Cleaning it may take a bit of time, especially if you have anchored in mud or clay. A bucket on the foredeck with a lanyard on it is very helpful to wash down the anchor and chain, which can bring aboard an amazing amount of smelly gunk.

5

TRAILER BASICS

Trailering a boat makes a lot of sense, because your choice of lakes and rivers is as far and varied as your rig can take you. A bonus is that you don't have to pay for permanent dock space.

One of the most attractive aspects of a small to midsize boat is that it is trailerable and can be transported over-land directly to the best boating areas. A three-hour drive down the coast with your boat in tow can put you in a new harbor that could take several days to reach by water. A short trek overland lets you explore new lakes, rivers, and waterways.

Basic trailering skills are not difficult to learn, and every time you tow your boat to a ramp, launch it, and retrieve it, you'll gain confidence and experience. Here are the basics about the right equipment and how to use it.

THE BASIC RIG

Trailerable boats come in all sizes, and so do their trailers. The trailer should be matched to the boat. All trailers have a weight capacity plate attached to them that specifies the maximum load capacity. The maximum load must include everything on the trailer, including the boat and all the gear stored inside it.

Generally, single-axle trailers designed for loads of less than 1,500 pounds are not too complicated. Trailer requirements vary state by state, but all states require at least tail, brake, and turn-signal lights. Safety chains are also required to prevent the trailer from dragging on the road and breaking loose if it comes off the hitch.

Heavier trailers require brakes, which can be either electric or hydraulic. Surge brakes use the momentum of the trailer to provide the braking force. When the brakes of the tow car are applied, the momentum of the trailer causes it to run up behind the car. This force is absorbed by a hydraulic cylinder on the trailer tow bar and used to apply the brakes, slowing the trailer. The harder the tow car brakes, the harder the trailer brakes are applied.

Smaller boats can be pulled by most properly equipped midsize or larger cars. Your car's towing capacity should be listed in the owner's manual; if it's not, ask the dealer. Inexpensive oil and transmission coolers can be added to most cars to increase their towing capacity and are well worth the small investment. Large boats can be towed behind properly equipped light trucks, vans, and four-wheel-drive sport utility vehicles.

A basic single-axle trailer for a light boat has tail, brake, and turn-signal lights, but does not require brakes. All trailers must have safety chains strung between the trailer and car hitch.

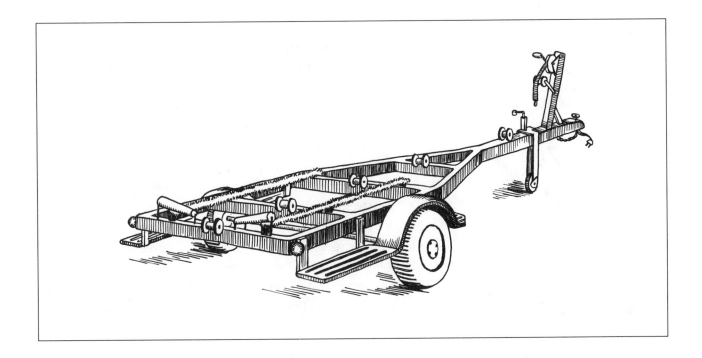

Always start backing with the trailer aligned with the car. When backing, grip the steering wheel at the bottom. Turning the car wheel clockwise causes the rear of the car to go right, swinging the trailer to the left.

TOWING A BOAT

Towing a boat is not difficult if you take just a few basic factors into consideration. First, the car and trailer combination is at least twice as long as the car you are used to driving. This extra length changes the handling characteristics of the car. You will have to make wider turns to prevent the trailer from running over the curb as it tries to follow the car. The extra trailer weight will slow the acceleration of the car and lengthen its stopping distance. A fully loaded trailer can double the distance it takes you to stop the car. If you take these facts into consideration when you are cornering, passing, and braking, you can safely tow just about any boat.

Spend a few minutes checking the load before you venture out on the road and you're more likely to have an uneventful trip. Check that loose items in the boat are secure. If you have a canvas cover, make sure it is tied down. If you are towing a sailboat, check that the mast and all the rigging are fastened and secured so they won't rub and chafe against one another and other parts of the boat.

Towing a boat puts added strain on the car, so proper maintenance of both car and trailer is important. Make sure the car is tuned up and running at its peak performance. See that wheel bearings on the trailer are greased and that car and trailer are running smoothly. Inspect all lights and turn signals. Ask someone to step on the brake pedal and operate the turn signals while you check that the lights are functioning. Take a careful look at the trailer hitch to see that it is locked in position and that the safety chains are crossed under the trailer hitch and attached to the car. Check the air pressure in the trailer tires and the car. Don't forget to inspect the spare tire for both the trailer and car.

Except when making wide turns, going forward with your rig is not much different from driving the car alone. Driving in reverse is another matter. Oversteering when backing up is usually the biggest mistake the first-time driver with a tow makes. Very little wheel movement is needed to make the trailer steer right or left, and too much wheel movement usually causes the trailer to jackknife.

The real trick to backing up a trailer is to pull forward far enough so the trailer and car are in alignment. Pull forward until the trailer is directly behind the car, then shift into reverse, and hold the steering wheel at the bottom. As you face forward, notice that when you move your hand to the left, you turn the steering wheel clockwise and the back of the car moves to the right and begins to swing the trailer to the left. If you move your hand to the right, the steering wheel turns counterclockwise and the trailer will swing right. The key is to go slow and use small movements of the wheel when steering the trailer.

Then, as you begin to back down the ramp, try to anticipate the trailer's movement. If it begins to turn, correct by turning the steering wheel so the back of your car moves toward the direction the trailer is turning. Go slow, so if you get confused and turn the wheel the wrong way, and the trailer begins to turn more sharply than expected, you have time to turn the wheel the other way to correct. Just remember to turn the rear of the car in the same direction that the trailer is turning to straighten it. If the trailer begins to turn too sharply and jackknifes, stop and pull forward to straighten it out.

Cars are not designed to operate at high speeds with a trailer, so whenever you are towing a boat, go easy on the accelerator. Almost all towing problems can be avoided if you slow down and take it easy. Driving at a steady 50–55 mph is easy on your car and tow.

If you drive up hill, downshift into a lower gear to allow the engine to develop more power. Be careful going downhill, because the added weight of the trailer will cause the car to gain speed. Pulling a tow you will descend on a steep grade faster than when driving the car alone. Brake often and for short periods to check the speed before it gets excessive. The pauses between braking will allow the brakes to cool so they maintain efficiency. It may take you three or four times the normal distance to stop your rig when going down a hill, so be prepared.

When passing another car or truck, allow yourself plenty of room to maneuver. Remember you have less acceleration and a much longer rig so it will take you considerably longer to pass.

LAUNCHING

Whether you are an old pro at trailering or a beginner, the secret to a no-hassle launch is preparation. Take time to check out the condition of the ramp and see how other skippers are launching their boats. Observe how far into the water they are backing their trailers to get an idea of the slope of the ramp and just how deep you will have to back into the water. This observation time gives the trailer wheels a chance to cool down, which is good, because backing into the water with hot wheel bearings can draw water into the hubs, something you want to avoid.

Most ramp areas have a parking area where you can stop and get your boat ready to launch. Remove the cover, tilt up the outboard motor or stern drive, and be sure to remove any wood blocks or braces used for extra support while towing. See the Launching Checklist on the next page for more details.

If you have a sailboat, rig its mast, but before you raise it, check for overhead power lines. Also check that there are no low power lines between your boat and the ramp.

Before you begin to back down the ramp, pull ahead and get the trailer lined up behind the car. Then back down the ramp slowly and stop just short of the water. Apply the parking brake and put the car in park or turn the engine off and leave the car in gear. Loosen the trailer cable and gather up the mooring lines for your crew to hold. Then slowly back into the water and launch the boat. Have the crew pull the boat out of the launch area and tie it up to the boarding-area dock while you park the car and trailer.

Launching Checklist
- Make sure drain plug is in place.
- Unplug trailer lights or remove trailer lights and stow.
- Make sure winch cable is tight and locked.
- Remove tiedowns and any stern-drive supports.

HAULING OUT

Retrieving your boat and hauling it up on the trailer is basically the reverse procedure of launching it. Take your time backing down the ramp and align the trailer perpendicular to the water, which makes it easier to align the boat on the trailer when you haul it out. Place the car in park with the parking break on or leave it in gear and turn the engine off if it is a standard shift. If you have a heavy boat (over 1,500 pounds), place a pair of wooden blocks behind the rear tires to help hold the car in place as you winch the boat up onto the trailer.

Take your time hauling the boat onto the trailer. Check that the boat is resting properly on the trailer and not listing to one side or out of alignment with the center rollers. It's easy to correct at this point, but once it's up out of the water, jockeying the boat around on the trailer is difficult, and downright impossible if it's a large craft. See the Haulout Checklist on the next page for more details.

Before you pull up the ramp make sure that the winch cable is tight and that you have at least the stern tie down in place and tight so the boat will not shift when going up the ramp. Use low gear to pull the boat up the ramp and go slow to maintain maximum traction.

When the boat and trailer are clear of the launch ramp, replace all the tie-downs and reinstall stern drive supports and trailer lights if they have been removed. Be sure to test the lights and grease the trailer hubs if they have been underwater before you hit the road.

Haulout Checklist

- Pack up garbage, food sacks, etc. and tidy up, securing anything loose.
- Allow outboard engine to idle with fuel line disconnected to empty engine of fuel.
- Tilt outboard or stern drive to up position.
- Secure fenders or other items that may get caught in the trailer during haulout.
- Place wheel blocks behind rear wheels of the tow car if you have a heavy boat.

6

WATERSKIING

The protected waters of inland lakes and rivers are ideal for waterskiing.

Skipping over the water on skis, a kneeboard, or a ski tube continues to grow as a popular water sport. For both the driver and the skier, there are skills to learn and practices to follow for safe going. Head for uncrowded waters with little or no wake whenever possible. Avoid swimming areas, low-speed mooring lanes, and marina channels. Don't ski near other boats, docks, or fishing areas, and ski with caution, not gay abandon.

Don't water-ski at night or early in the morning where you might disturb other boaters at anchor or people ashore. And don't ski in unfamiliar waters, which may have tree stumps or sandbars you don't know about. As both skier and driver, give a wide berth to fishermen or slow-moving boats such as canoes and kayaks.

The boat should be equipped with a wide-angle rearview mirror and a pylon that holds the towline above the motor and helps prevent the line from becoming entangled in the propeller. The pylon gives safer access to the towline from within the boat.

Two people are required in a boat for safe waterskiing conditions—a driver and an observer who can communicate with the skier, using hand signals. The standard waterskiing signals appear below and are explained on the next page.

These hand signals to help a skier and driver communicate are recommended by the American Water Ski Association.

Go Faster

Go Slower

Stop

Signals Presence to Other Boats

Tells Boat to Go Right

Tells Boat to Go Left

OK After Fall

Shut Off Boat Engine

Return to Shore

- Thumb up means speed up.
- Thumb down means slow down.
- Opened hand means stop.
- One finger up or an arm extended means turn.
- Hand flat overhead means go back to the dock.
- Finger under chin means cut the motor.
- Both hands clasped together overhead after a fall mean you're okay.

To be a safe water-skier you should be a good swimmer and wear a Type III PFD designated as a ski vest. The vest should fit snugly, because if it's loose and moves around easily and you fall, it could slide up on your body, pinning an arm against your body, or it could come off in a bad fall.

Choose skis or a kneeboard with rounded edges and no protrusions. Fins should be blunt-edged rather than sharp. Binders or binding straps should be comfortable and free of rough buckles. In general, skis for youngsters should be about 40–50 inches long and those for adults should be 60–70 inches long. The towline is usually 75 feet long, including the handle. Store the towline in an enclosed area, because it can weaken when exposed to the sun.

If you are the driver, allow for the skier's ability by adjusting the speed of the boat. Before turning the boat, look to both sides and behind to make sure there are no other boats that might endanger the skier. Remember that the skier at the end of the towline is an extension of the boat.

If the skier goes down, return to him quickly and pass him slowly, pulling the towline past him so he can take hold of it. When the skier wants to get aboard, pull in the towline and approach him slowly from downwind. Always keep the skier clearly visible and on the driver's side of the boat. Turn off the motor when taking a skier aboard from the water.

When you're the skier in the water, hold up one of the skis so other boaters and your driver know your location.

If you're operating a boat near a boat pulling a water-skier, stay as far away from the skier as possible, because if the skier falls he might be in your path.

SAILING BASICS

Sailing sometimes appears a lot more difficult and complicated than it really is. Making a boat move through the water by wind power alone is not difficult—in fact, every boat made will drift along with the wind if left to itself. This is fine if you want to go in the direction that the wind is blowing, and for centuries that is just about what early sailors did. Over time

Whether it's a small one-design sailboat for a solo sailor or a larger boat that requires crew members, sailing remains a popular sport with young and old sailors alike.

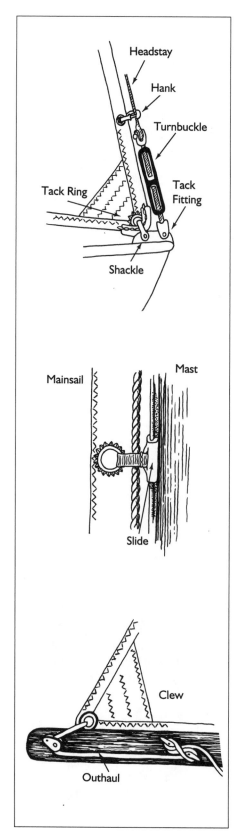

The basic parts of a small sailboat's rig are illustrated on this and the facing page. These basic components are found on almost any sailboat.

and with much trial and error, sailing developed into its present form, incorporating the ancient art tempered with high-tech science.

Basic sailing skills can be learned in a few hours on the water, but to master the sport can take a lifetime and then some. For many sailors the challenge is the attraction of sailing. With a little bit of study and practice, you can learn to sail a boat in most conditions, and this basic knowledge will let you enjoy the sport to any degree you want.

SAILING AND ITS LANGUAGE

Probably the most intimidating aspect of sailing is the language used to describe it. Sailing as we know it today evolved over centuries. Large sailing ships of earlier eras had hundreds of ropes that were

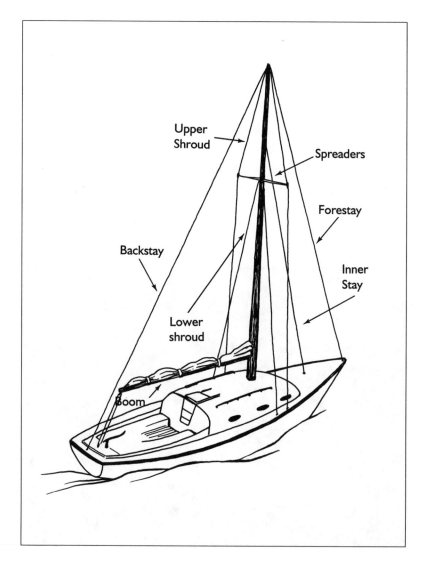

used to control the ship and sails. An exact vocabulary developed so sailors could communicate. Many of these terms are rather descriptive and give a clue to their meaning, such as "foot," which means the bottom edge of a sail. But some terms, like "clew," the bottom outboard corner of a sail, don't give you a clue!

Before you get bogged down in the terminology, take a look at the illustration of the basic parts of a small one-design type of sailboat. These are the basic parts of any sailboat. Most parts of a sailboat that have to do with sailing can be grouped into four basic categories: mast and boom; standing rigging; sails; and running rigging.

MAST AND BOOM

All sailboats have a mast to support the sails. The most common type of rig for boats under 30 feet is the sloop rig, which has a single mast, usually made from an aluminum extrusion. The simplest example of this is the short freestanding mast on a Laser. This small boat's mast fits into a sturdy socket in the deck. No other support is needed, so the sail can be attached to the mast with a sleeve that is slipped over the mast. Of course, the other extreme is the mast of a large ocean racer, which can be almost 100 feet tall and must be supported by a virtual forest of cables.

Attached to the aft end of the mast is a horizontal aluminum or wooden member called the boom. The bottom edge of the sail is attached to it so it can be controlled by a rope tackle called the main sheet. This allows the sailor to control the shape of the sail and to position the boom relative to the centerline of the boat so the sail presents itself most efficiently to the wind.

STANDING RIGGING

To keep the mast upright, most sailboats have a system of wires called standing rigging. The most important of these wires support the mast. On most boats a wire cable called the forestay runs from the bow of the boat to the top or, in some cases, partway up the front of the mast. An opposing wire, the backstay, runs from the masthead to the stern of the boat. The forestay and backstay keep the mast from moving forward or backward.

Another set of wires run from the masthead over a set of

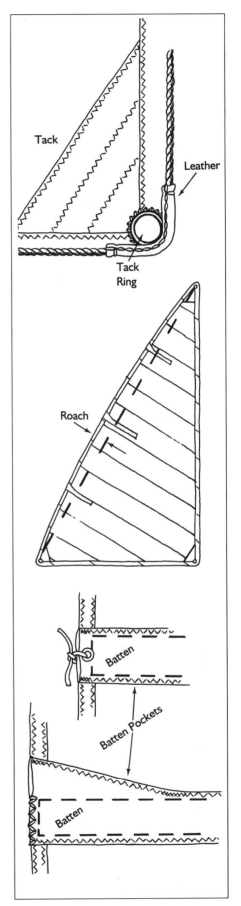

spreaders about three-quarters of the way up the mast to either side of the boat and are called the upper shrouds. The spreaders expand the angle between the upper shrouds and the masthead, increasing their leverage. These shrouds prevent the mast from moving to port or starboard.

On some types of designs there is a set of lower shrouds, usually attached to the mast at the spreaders, that lead to the deck to help control the bend of the mast.

The tension on these cables, or running rigging, is adjusted with screw turnbuckles or other devices. By adjusting the tension of forestay, backstay, and upper and lower shrouds, the mast can be made to stand straight or bend slightly to help shape the sails. There is an endless variety of rig designs, but most of them have these basic elements.

SAILS

Most modern sails are made from synthetic materials, usually Dacron or nylon. Sails on racing boats or larger sailboats are often reinforced with other fabrics, namely Mylar and Kevlar. These lightweight but extremely strong fabrics give a sail the ability to hold its shape through a wide range of wind conditions. These materials are ideal sail fabrics, because they don't stretch or absorb water, and best of all, they won't rot or be damaged by mildew. Even though sails are tough, they do need care. Mildew won't rot a sail, but it will stain it. And a sail can self-destruct if left exposed to the sunlight.

Each part of a sail has a particular name. Sloops have a triangular-shaped mainsail and jib. The sail usually referred to as the main is attached to the back edge of the mast. Some boats have a track fastened to the mast for metal slides that are sewn or lashed to the forward edge, or luff, of the mainsail. Others, especially on smaller boats, have a groove in the back of the mast where a bolt rope is fed through. This rope is sewn to the luff of the mainsail.

The halyard is attached to the head of the sail so it can be hoisted up the mast. The opposite lower corner of the sail is called the tack and is fastened to the boom.

The bottom edge of the mainsail, called its foot, is attached to the boom in the same way as the main. It can also be left free or loose-footed. The outer lower corner of the sail is called its clew and is attached to an outhaul. The outhaul pulls the corner of the sail toward the end of the boom. Tightening the outhaul pulls the clew toward the end of the boom, stretching the foot tight and flattening the sail. Loosening the outhaul allows the sail to take on a fuller shape. Tightening the halyard has the same effect on the luff or forward edge of the main.

The free edge of the mainsail is called its roach. This edge is usually not cut along a straight line between the clew and head like the other two edges. It is rounded to give the sail a little extra area. To keep this extra material from flapping in the breeze, wood or plastic battens are used for support.

The jib is the sail on the bow forward of the main, and its corners have the same names as the corners of the main. The tack of the jib is attached to the deck just behind the forestay. The luff is attached to the forestay with sail hanks. Some boats have a grooved plastic or aluminum extrusion fitted over the forestay that the jib luff slides into. These extrusions can be controlled by sail-furling gear that allows you to roll up the jib like a large window shade.

The jib is hoisted with its own halyard connected to the head of the sail. Jib sheets are lines that are tied or clipped to the clew and lead to port and starboard cleats or winches on either side of the boat.

RUNNING RIGGING

The ropes that control the sails are called running rigging. Clipper ships had hundreds of sail-control ropes, but modern sailboats have only a few. In order to haul the sails up the mast, sailboats have a set of lines or wire ropes called halyards. The main halyard hauls up the mainsail, and the jib halyard hoists the jib. These sheets are usually secured to cleats on the mast or on larger boats are controlled by winches on the mast or deck. Each sail that is hoisted requires a halyard, so many boats have several jib and other special-purpose halyards, such as the spinnaker halyard, used to hoist the large colorful sail used for sailing downwind.

In addition to halyards, sailboats use sheets to control the shape and set of the sails. The two primary control sheets are the main and jib. The mainsheet is usually a multipart tackle attached to the boom and deck that controls the movement of the boom. Letting line out or easing the mainsheet allows the boom to move away from the centerline of the boat. Trimming, or pulling it in, moves the boom and mainsail closer to the centerline.

The jibsheet is attached to the clew, or lower corner, of the jib and runs through a block on deck and then to a cleat or winch. Trimming the jibsheet pulls the corner of the sail back, stretching it and making it flatter. Easing the sheet lets the corner move forward, allowing the sail to assume a fuller shape.

▲ ▲ ▲

HANGING HALYARDS ON CLEAT ON THE MAST

When the sail is hoisted, the long halyard tail can be a nuisance on deck, so store it on its mast cleat. Coil the line with a foot or so left free between the mast cleat and the coil. Then reach through the coil and pull the short section of halyard through the coil and twist it three or four times on itself to create a loop. Hook the loop over the horn of the cleat to hold the halyard in place.

▼ ▼ ▼

HOW A SAIL WORKS

The aerodynamics of sailing is a very complicated subject, but a little basic understanding of how wind affects sails is all that it takes to actually make a sailboat sail. Depending on the direction the sailboat is traveling relative to the wind, sails may look like an airplane's wing or like a loose bag catching the wind.

If you watch a sailboat on a broad reach or run with its boom let out until it is almost touching the shrouds, it is not too difficult to figure out how sails power the boat—they catch the wind like an umbrella on a windy day! However, it is not so obvious how these same sails work when they are shaped like an airplane's wing and are pulling the boat upwind. Determining how to trim and shape the sails is an art, but the basics are not difficult to grasp. Of course, you can't discuss sail trim without first defining the relation between a boat and the wind.

A sailboat can sail through about 270 degrees. The points of sail include close-hauled, reaching, and running.

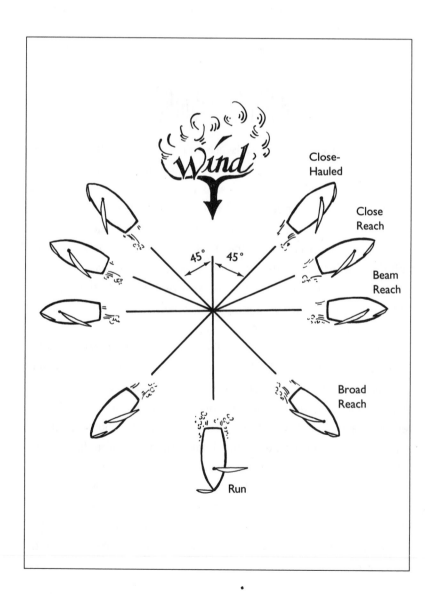

THE WIND AND YOUR BOAT

Let's use for an example a sailboat with an outboard motor. It's a calm day with no wind. The flag flying at the marina lies limp, because there is no wind to move it. You head out under power and feel a slight breeze coming from the bow. The boat moving through the still air creates its own wind.

Later in the day, a light 5-knot breeze fills in from the south. At the same time you are motoring south at 5 knots. You will notice an increase in the wind from 5 knots to 10 knots. In this situation it is easy to see that the boat speed and wind speed work together to produce an apparent 10-knot wind. Apparent wind is the direction and force of the wind relative to the boat, and it varies with the speed and direction of the boat. As you turn north to go back to the marina, the wind seems to die down to almost nothing. That's because you are motoring north at 5 knots and the wind is blowing north at 5 knots so the apparent wind around your boat does not seem to be blowing.

Actually, it's pretty easy to figure out the apparent wind if you are going directly into the wind or directly away from it, but it's not so obvious if you are sailing at other angles. Since the sails only experience the apparent wind, you really don't have to be too concerned with the true wind, but it is important to understand that the movement of the boat through the water affects the direction and strength of the apparent wind and that the true wind can be considerably different from the wind hitting the sailor's face.

As a boat sails closer into the wind from abeam to dead ahead, the apparent wind is increased and moved farther forward than the true wind. The apparent wind moves aft and is weaker than the true wind the farther a boat steers from abeam the wind to dead aft.

Here's an example. You are sailing downwind with your boat going through the water at about 6 knots with the apparent wind at your back. If the breeze blowing over your boat feels like a stiff 15 knots on this point of sail, you should be ready to face at least 20-to-25-knot winds when you tack and turn to sail home. Going downwind, the speed of your boat reduces the apparent wind, but sailing upwind, your boat speed will increase it.

WIND AND SAILS

Unlike a boat under power, a sailboat is limited in the direction it can go. A sailboat depends on the interaction of the wind and sails for power, and sails can't produce useful power through the whole

360-degree range that a boat can maneuver. No sailboat can sail directly into the wind, but a modern design boat can usually sail within 45 degrees of the true wind, which is the actual direction and force of the wind. It can function efficiently through about 270 degrees of the possible 360 degrees available. By tacking upwind and jibing downwind, a sailboat can reach any destination.

A boat sailing as close to upwind as possible is close-hauled, beating to windward, or simply beating. As the boat bears away from the true wind, it is close-reaching, and then as the wind becomes abeam the boat it is beam-reaching. Heading farther downwind, a boat is broad-reaching until the wind moves well aft; then it is running.

A boat can sail on any of these points of sail on either a port or starboard tack. A boat is on a starboard tack when the wind is blowing over the starboard rail and the boom is on the port side. The opposite is true for a port tack.

When close-hauled or beating, a sailboat can't sail directly into the wind, so to reach a destination directly upwind of it, it must sail in a series of steps, first on one tack, then on the other. Sailing from one of these steps to the other is called tacking. The boat is steered into the wind, and as soon as the bow passes through the wind so it is blown off on the opposite side, the sails are retrimmed. The boat continues turning until the sails fill and it can continue on the new tack.

When sailing downwind, a boat is jibed onto a new tack. In this maneuver the stern of the boat is brought through the wind and the main boom swings over to the other side of the boat as the wind passes from dead astern to the other side of the boat.

SAILING CLOSE-HAULED

Sailing a boat upwind is probably the most challenging point of sail, because on a beat the sails are trimmed in tight and take on an airfoil shape that permits them to develop lift, like the wing of an airplane. Take, for example, the jib of a boat beating to windward. As the wind passes over the sail, the leading edge of the sail divides the flow of air into two streams. One passes in front of the sail, or to windward, and the other passes behind the sail, to leeward. Because of the curved airfoil shape of the sail, the air passing to leeward must travel a bit farther than the stream to weather. Since the two streams of air rejoin at the aft edge or leach of the sail, the leeward stream must travel faster to cover the extra distance. The accelerated airflow on the leeward side of the sail creates a low-pressure area, driving the boat along its leading edge.

Unfortunately, lift is not the only force created by the wind blowing over the sails. The wind pressure against the sail creates a heeling force and considerable sideways force at the same time it is creating lift. The heeling force is counteracted by the weight of the boat's keel or by your body weight placed on the windward side of the boat. The sideways force is counteracted by the keel or centerboard, which is shaped like an airfoil so it can produce lift when it moves through the water. These forces work against each other, but if the sails are properly trimmed the results will create enough lift to move the boat forward.

The key words here are "sail trim." The more lift the sail can create, the greater the forward driving forces will be. Like the wing of an airplane, all airfoils have an optimum shape and angle of attack. The shape of a sail is basically determined by the sailmaker, but small, important shape changes are possible when sailing. The angle of attack or the angle that the leading edge of the sail forms with the oncoming air is controlled by trimming the sheets or steering the boat.

Since you have the most control over the sail's angle of attack, let's look at these controls first. In order for the sail to develop lift, there has to be a smooth airflow over both sides of the sail. Since

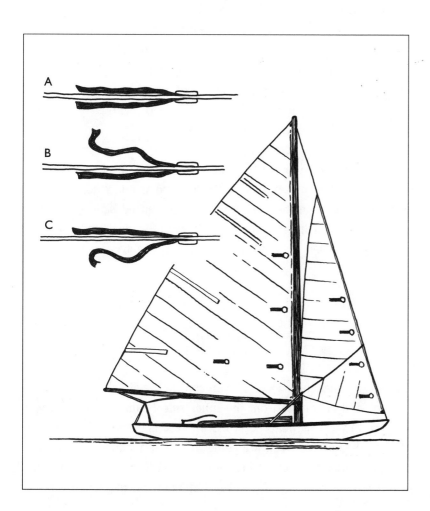

Telltales are short strips of plastic or yarn on each side of the sail used to help trim the sails for the best performance. When both stream evenly (A), the sail is properly trimmed; when the windward lifts (B), the sail needs to be trimmed; and when the leeward lifts (C), the sail should be let out.

the airflow can be bent only a small amount before it begins to become turbulent, the sail must be trimmed so its angle of attack is not too great, but is great enough to create lift.

If the sail is not trimmed in enough or the boat is steered into the wind too far, the angle of attack of the sail is so small that it does not create any lift and the sail is said to be luffing. A luffing sail will shake along its leading edge in windy conditions and pucker a little in light air. If the sail is trimmed in too far or the boat is not sailed into the wind enough, the sail will appear full but will create more heeling and sideways force than lift.

The easiest way to tell if you have the sail trimmed properly is to use telltales. They are short strips of plastic or yarn on each side of the sail placed 6 to 12 inches back from its luff and a few feet above the deck in the middle of the sail and toward its top. When the air is not flowing smoothly over the sail, the turbulence causes them to flutter.

For example, if the boat is sailed too close into the wind, the windward telltale will begin to lift, since the angle of attack is too low. In this situation, either steer the boat away from the wind, which is called falling off, or trim the sail. If the leeward or outside telltale flutters, either steer the boat closer to the wind, which is called heading up, or ease the sail.

These are general concepts and should be applied to your particular sailboat. Finding the best trim point for your boat will take some experimentation. Start sailing with your jib trimmed in until it is almost touching the spreaders and the mainsail trimmed in until the boom is almost on the centerline of the boat. Then steer the boat by the telltales.

If it is windy, you will probably have to ease the main so the boat doesn't heel too much or develop steering problems. Experiment with different settings of the jib and main. When going to weather, just remember that most inexperienced sailors overtrim their sails, especially in light air. Try to keep the inside telltale lifting a little as you sail to weather, since it is probably your fastest sail setting.

TACKING

Tacking is a maneuver in which you change the direction of the boat so the wind is coming from the other side of the boat. When you prepare to tack the boat, don't rush things. Make sure the crew are ready and know that you are going to tack. Announce that you are going to start tacking by saying, "Ready about," or "Prepare to tack." Your crew should respond, "Ready." Standing on the windward side

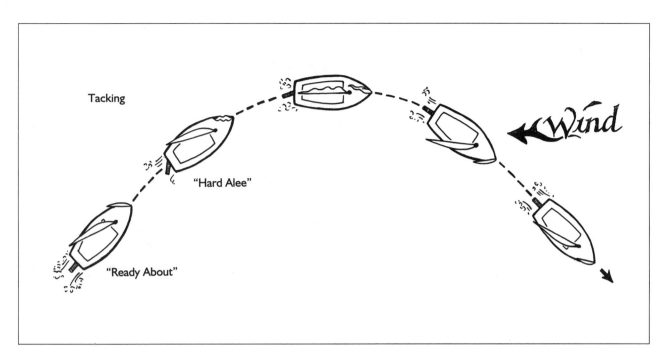

Tacking

"Hard Alee"

"Ready About"

Wind

of the boat, push the tiller away from you to start the turn into the wind. Make the first part of the turn fast and decisive, but slow the turn as the boat comes head to wind to allow time for the jib to move from one tack to the other. Keep the boat turning so it will move through the eye of the wind. Once the bow has passed through the wind, steer away from the wind slowly to allow the crew to trim the jib. Then come up to a new course and continue beating. On most sailboats less than 30 feet, the skipper controls the helm and mainsheet and a crew member tends the jib sheet.

Each boat responds differently when tacking. A light boat will slow faster, so you may have to turn her through the wind quicker than a heavy boat with lots of momentum. Also, tacking will be different in strong and light air. Practicing with your crew is the only way to get to know how your boat will respond in different conditions.

To tack a boat, head up into the wind. When the sail luffs, release it and continue turning the boat through the eye of the wind. Then trim the sails on the opposite side of the boat.

REACHING

As you steer your boat away from the wind, you are no longer beating, you're on a close reach. As you sail farther off the wind, you will be on a beam reach when the wind is abeam and on a broad reach when the wind is just aft of abeam.

These points of sail usually allow you to sail directly toward your destination, so it is easier to sail a straight course and trim the sail to the wind. The farther off the wind you sail, the more your sails must be eased for them to develop lift.

Use the telltales to trim the sails. Before you adjust anything, settle on the course you want to steer. Then take a look at the telltales on the jib. If the inner telltale is lifting, trim the sail; if the outer telltale is lifting, ease it.

When the jib is set, trim the mainsail. As you ease the mainsheet, the boom has a tendency to lift, allowing the top of the sail to develop excessive twist. To prevent this, most boats have a boom vang to help hold down the boom. On smaller boats this is usually a block and tackle rigged between the boom and the base of the mast.

On a reach or run, pull the boom vang tight enough to prevent the boom from lifting. Experiment with the vang setting. If you pull it too tight in windy conditions, some boats will develop excess weather helm, which is a tendency to turn into the wind. If you constantly have to fight the helm to keep your boat on course, especially in the puffs, try easing the vang.

SAILING DOWNWIND

Once the wind has moved towards the stern, you are said to be sailing downwind. This is probably the easiest point of sail, since you are moving with the wind and waves. Remember that the speed of your boat reduces the apparent wind, so going downwind on a light-wind day can be very slow sailing. Of course, the opposite is true if the wind is really blowing. Sailing downwind in heavy air can be very exciting and challenging. The following waves have a tendency to lift the stern, making steering difficult. If you don't maintain control, the boat could jibe, and in heavy air the boom comes crashing dangerously across the boat and can give you a nasty headache or break the boom or mast.

Jibing is the reverse of tacking. The stern passes through the eye of the wind as the boat changes direction.

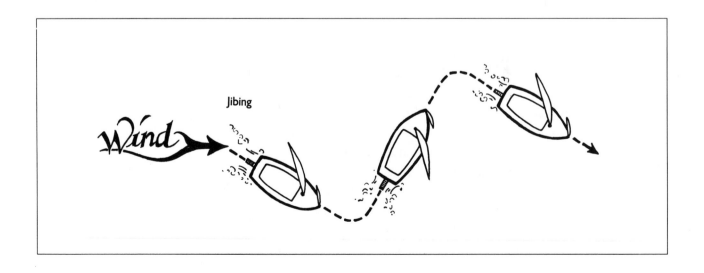

Jibing

Wind

In order to sail from one downwind tack to another, the boat is jibed. Except on windy days, jibing a boat is not difficult if everyone is ready. Even on light-wind days an unexpected jibe should be avoided. Since the boat is sailing downwind, the boom is let out, so during a jibe the boom travels from one side of the boat to the other and can pick up a lot of momentum.

Jibing is the reverse of tacking upwind, since the stern passes through the eye of the wind. Just as when tacking, the helmsman should warn the crew that the boat is about to jibe by stating, "Prepare to jibe."

When the crew are ready, steer the boat dead downwind and in light air grab the mainsheet and state, "Jibing," or "Jibe ho." Then pull the main through the wind onto the new tack. Then slowly steer toward the wind as the jib is being brought around and trimmed on the opposite side. Keep heading up until the jib fills and the jibe is complete.

You have the most control over the tiller during the jibe if you stand on the new tack's upwind side. For example, when you are on a port tack with wind blowing over the port side and the boom out to starboard, move to the starboard side of the tiller just before the jibe. When the boat heels over on the new tack, you will be on the high side and able to apply leverage to the tiller.

In medium air you want to prevent the boom from flying across the boat, because it is dangerous for crew and skipper and can damage the mainsheet. Before you begin to jibe, haul in on the mainsheet until the main is well in. Check that the mainsheet is free to run, jibe the boat, and let the mainsheet run free to act as a shock absorber.

If the wind is really blowing, avoid jibing altogether. Instead, head up into the wind and tack your boat. It will take a little longer, but tacking in windy conditions is a much more controlled and hence a safer maneuver.

8

WEATHER

hat's it going to be like for the weekend?" is the weather question most asked by boaters. Every outdoor activity revolves around the forecast, and boating is no exception. The weather forecast and boating opportunities go hand in hand, because on the water, boaters are vulnerable to changes in the temperature, wind conditions, and approaching weather fronts.

A weather front forms as different air masses collide, and it gets its name from the type of air that is moving into the area. For example, cold air coming in from the north that collides with warm air forms a cold front. The dense cold air pushes under the warm air and lifts it, creating stormy weather. When warm air collides with cool conditions, it's a warm front that pushes warm air up and over the cooler air. A warm front usually is less severe than a cold front.

A cold front is often preceded by a squall line of threatening clouds and storms with sudden wind shifts. These conditions are usually followed by rain, and then a clearing with cool clear weather.

A warm front is signaled by a drop in barometric pressure with thickening clouds. The wind shifts clockwise and then decreases in strength. Warmer temperatures are followed by clear skies and a return to normal winds.

Thunderstorms are a fair indicator of a change in the weather

▲ ▲ ▲
FOGGY CONDITIONS

When a fog rolls in over the water, the conditions are often called "pea soup" because of the thick air that seems to hang in the atmosphere. Fog is often the result of warm, humid air settling over cooler water or land. When navigating a boat in these conditions, go slow so you can hear other boats, waves breaking on the shore, and foghorns or other aids like bell or whistle buoys. Periodically turn your engine off and you'll be amazed at the sounds you can hear, which may give you some clue to your location.

▼ ▼ ▼

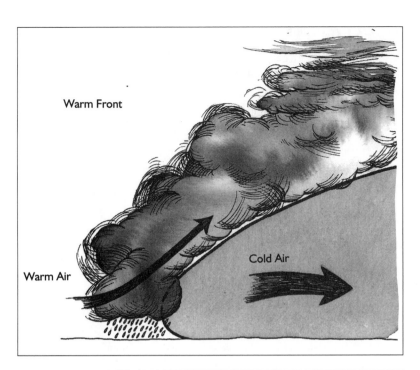

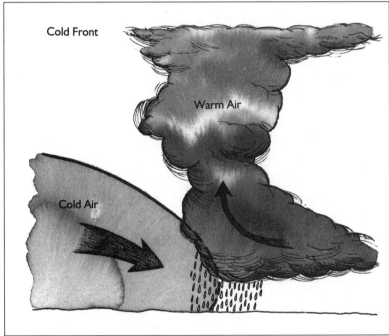

A warm front occurs when warm air collides with cold conditions and the warm air is pushed up and over the cold air. A cold front is caused when cold air collides with warm air, pushing under the warm air and lifting it, creating stormy weather.

pattern. They often appear quickly out of a cloudless sky or hidden in a hazy sky. They are caused by rising air currents going from warm to cool in a short period of time. Heavy rain or hail develops, cooling the air inside the clouds.

Boaters should keep a weather eye particularly on hot hazy afternoons, when thunderstorms frequently occur. Be on the lookout for signs of lightning, listen for the sound of thunder, and be mindful that there's often a lull in the wind before the storm hits.

While you're under way, listen to the radio weather broadcast at regular intervals to learn of any changes and keep a weather eye for dark threatening clouds and an increase in wind or sea conditions. NOAA weather is broadcast on the VHF radio with about a 40-mile range. The broadcasts are on WX-1, WX-2, and WX-3 frequencies.

When you hear a clap of lightning or see a lightning flash, you can guesstimate how far you are from the ensuing storm. Count the number of seconds between the flash and the clap and divide by five, which tells you the number of miles you are from the storm. For example, if the time lapse is fifteen seconds, divide by five; the storm is approximately 3 miles away from you.

The longer the time interval between the lightning flash and thunderclap, the farther the storm is from you. Sometimes there is so much lightning in the general area that this may not be a reliable indication of the time you have before the storm hits. But if the interval between the lightning flash and thunderclap is getting shorter, then you can be pretty sure the storm is moving in your direction. In any case, if you see lightning or hear thunder, head for port or sheltered waters; or if you think the storm will hit before you can get back to port, prepare your boat for the approaching storm.

Storm signals are often flown at public docks and boat clubs to advise you about the weather conditions. A small craft advisory is a red triangular flag warning that wind speed will be up to 38 knots, which creates dangerous conditions for small boats.

A gale warning is two red triangular flags, one flying above the other, warning that wind speed will be from 39 to 54 knots.

A storm warning is a square red flag with a black square in the center, warning of winds between 55 and 73 knots. Two square red flags with black square centers flying one above the other warns of winds exceeding 74 knots.

Storm warning flags for small craft advise boaters at public docks and marinas about weather conditions.

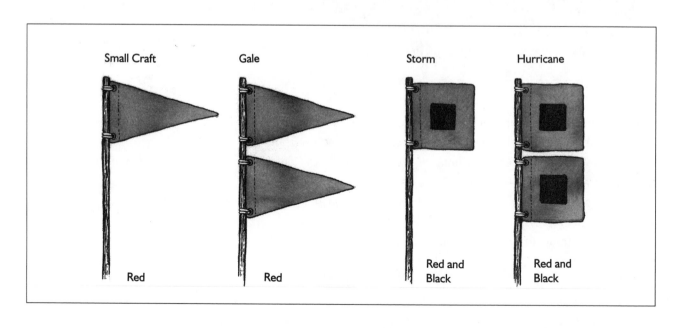

Small Craft	Gale	Storm	Hurricane
Red	Red	Red and Black	Red and Black

THUNDERSTORM

If you are caught in a thunderstorm, check that everyone aboard is wearing a life jacket and carefully tighten and secure all loose gear, ports, and hatches. Ask everyone aboard to keep a sharp lookout for other boats or obstructions.

When you're out and a thunderstorm hits, head into the wind by maneuvering the boat so it takes the first and heaviest gusts of winds on the bow, not abeam. If you are in a sailboat, get the sails down and secure them below, or tie them up so they can't flap wildly in the wind. If you have a powerboat or a sailboat with engine, steer a course so you approach waves at a 45-degree angle. This will reduce the pounding and give you a more comfortable and safer ride. Taking the waves at an angle will also help keep the propeller in the water if your boat is powered by an outboard motor.

If you are in a small sailboat without an engine, you should of course get the sail down. You won't be able to keep the bow into the waves without power, so steer your boat downwind and ride with the wind and waves. Get the anchor ready, and if you approach shore or some other danger, toss it out even if you are in deep water. It will slow your boat and in most cases will eventually catch on the bottom as the water begins to shoal.

If you're on the water and lightning is visible, keep away from metal objects that are not grounded to the boat's protection system. Stay low in the boat so you're not a target.

▲ ▲ ▲

WIND SPEED

Just how hard is the wind blowing? If you don't have a wind-speed indicator aboard use this table to make an educated guess.

Wind Speed	Wave Condition
1–3	Ripples, no visible waves
4–6	Small waves forming, no whitecaps
7–10	Larger waves forming, few whitecaps
11–16	1-to-3-foot waves, frequent whitecaps
17–20	Larger waves, many whitecaps, some spray blowing off wave tops

▼ ▼ ▼

9

KNOTS

A bowline is one of the most useful knots, because it holds securely yet can be easily loosened even after it has been under great strain.

T here are few basic knots that will help you in boating. For many people, tying knots doesn't come easy. Practice tying them until you know you can do it right. Here's a rundown of the most-used knots with illustrations of how to tie them.

BOWLINE

Since it can be made quickly and loosened easily even after it has been under load, the bowline is the one knot every sailor should know. Use this knot to tie a jib line to a sail or to make a looped end on a dock line so you can drop it over a piling.

CLOVE HITCH

Most often used to secure a line to a piling while docking, the clove hitch is easy to tie and has good holding power when tied to a round post. It is not a secure knot and can eventually work loose.

If you are leaving your boat unattended, secure the clove hitch at each piling by throwing a couple of half hitches between the tail of the line and the line under load. This knot is also handy for hanging fenders from lifelines or stanchions.

FIGURE 8

Sailors use this simple stopper knot to make sure a sheet doesn't run out of a block. This knot will not jam and is easy to untie even after is has been under strain.

HALF HITCHES

This is a very fast knot to tie. You can increase the holding power of the hitch by wrapping two turns of line around whatever you are tying. This knot is also handy for hanging fenders or a fender board from lifelines and for securing a fender to a piling.

A clove hitch is used frequently to secure a line to a piling because it is quick to tie.

Far left: On sailboats a figure 8 is often used at the end of a sheet to keep it from running out of a block.

Left: Two half hitches will secure a fender or a fender board on a lifeline.

LINE HANDLING

To keep a line organized and ready to use, wrap it in a coil and loop the end of the line through and around the coil.

To keep lines straight and always ready to use, store them coiled. To coil a line, hold one end of the line in your hand and use your other hand to gather the line into uniform loops wound in a clockwise direction to prevent the line from twisting. When 18 to 20 inches of line remain, wrap this line at least twice around the upper third of the coil, then form a loop with the remaining line and pass it through the top portion of the coil. Pull the loop over the top of the coil and then give a tug to the end of the line to tighten the loop and hold the coil tight.

To heave a line to someone such as a dock tender, divide the coiled line into two parts. Hold a coil in your left hand, check to see that the other coil is long enough to reach the dock, then throw it with your right hand in one long sweeping movement.

To throw a line to someone, divide a coiled line in half, hold one section coiled in your left hand, and heave the other section with your right hand.

Keep lines on the dock or on deck orderly by coiling the ends in a spiral. It's called flemishing the lines. Straighten out the end of the line and wrap the end around itself until the line creates a flat spiral mat.

Flemish the loose end of a line on deck and on shore so it is wrapped around itself to form a flat spiral.

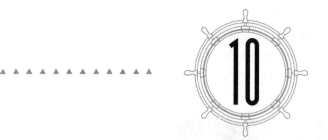

LAWS AND REQUIREMENTS FOR SAFE BOATING

Federal laws mandate certain safety equipment and operating procedures. Here are the basics of what you need to know to assure safe and legal boating.

REGISTRATION AND CERTIFICATE OF NUMBER

You're required to register a boat in the state where it is primarily used and have aboard the certificate of number, issued when registered, whenever the boat is being used. The number must be displayed on both sides of the forward half of the boat. Some states require a validation sticker, which is applied next to the set of numbers. Check with your local department of natural resources or state boating authority about the requirements in your state. In many states it's necessary to register on a yearly basis, and there is usually a fee.

You must notify the agency that issued the certificate of number if the boat is sold or transferred, destroyed, abandoned, lost, stolen, or recovered. Also notify the agency if the certificate of number is lost or destroyed or if the owner's address changes.

Some larger boats may be documented, which is a form of

federal or national registration. Documenting does not relieve the owner of paying any property tax or sales tax or state registration fees on the boat.

LAW ENFORCEMENT

A boat that is under way and is hailed by a Coast Guard vessel is required to heave to, or maneuver in such a manner that a boarding officer can come aboard. You should know the boarding policy and procedure of your state's marine law enforcement agency, too.

The Coast Guard may impose a civil penalty up to $1,000 for failure to comply with equipment requirements, report a boating accident, or comply with other federal regulations.

Operating a boat while intoxicated is prohibited. And negligent or grossly negligent operation of a boat that endangers life and/or property is prohibited.

All boating accidents must be reported to the proper marine law enforcement authority for the state where the accident occurred. Immediate notification is required for fatal accidents or if there are injuries requiring more than first aid.

Also a formal report must be made within ten days for accidents involving more than $500 damage or complete loss of a vessel. For more information about accident reporting, call the Boating Safety Hotline, 1 (800) 368-5647.

The person in charge of a boat is obligated by law to provide assistance that can be safely provided to any individual in danger at sea.

EQUIPMENT REQUIREMENTS

The equipment aboard your boat must comply with the Federal Equipment Requirements. The Coast Guard sets these minimum equipment standards so they comply with specifications and regulations relating to performance, construction, and materials.

PERSONAL FLOTATION DEVICES

These devices, also called PFDs, range from throwable buoyant cushions to float coats and vests and life jackets. In emergencies on the water it doesn't matter if you're a champion swimmer, what counts

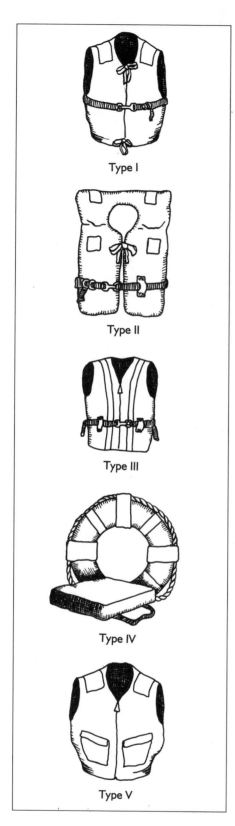

Types of personal flotation devices (PFDs):
Type I offshore life jacket; Type II near-shore
buoyant vest; Type III float coat or fishing
vest flotation aid; Type IV throwable device;
Type V hybrid with an inflatable chamber.

is your ability to stay afloat. You are required to carry one Coast Guard–approved PFD of the correct size and in good condition for each person aboard. PFDs are designed to keep you afloat until you are rescued and can help protect you from the fatal effects of cold weather.

Boats under 16 feet in length and canoes and kayaks of any length must be equipped with one Type I, II, III, IV, or V PFD for each person aboard.

Boats 16 feet and larger must be equipped with one Type I, II, III, or V PFD for each person aboard plus one Type IV.

These PFDs should be stowed so they are easy to find and readily accessible for use, not still in package wrappers or stuck in a compartment covered with other gear. There are five types of PFD, each designed for different boating activities and water conditions.

Type I PFD, the offshore life jacket, provides the most buoyancy and is designed to turn most unconscious wearers in the water to a face-up position. It is effective for open, rough water, even for prolonged periods of time. It offers the best protection, but is the most uncomfortable and bulky.

Type II PFD, the near-shore buoyant vest, will turn some unconscious wearers to face-up position in the water. It is intended for use in calm inland waters where there's a good chance of a quick rescue. These are more comfortable but less buoyant than Type I and are good for dinghy sailing and racing.

Type III PFD, the flotation aid, is a float coat or fishing vest for calm inland waters when the wearer is conscious and can maintain flotation while waiting for a quick rescue. These are not suitable for extended survival in rough water. They are recommended for activities such as waterskiing, canoeing, kayaking, and operating personal watercraft and for supervised activities such as dinghy races.

Type IV PFD is the throwable, not-wearable device for use in calm inland waters with heavy boat traffic. The device is a buoyant cushion or ring or horseshoe buoy that the person in the water holds on to until he is rescued.

Type V hybrid PFD relies on an inflatable tube for most of its buoyancy. Since the tube lies flat until inflated, this type of device is very comfortable to wear. When the tube is inflated, a Type V device has the same performance as a Type I. Cold-weather survival suits designed for hypothermia protection and float coats fall in this category. Type V devices must be worn while under way to be acceptable.

A water-skier is required to wear a PFD designed to withstand the impact of hitting the water at high speed. "Impact Class" marking on the label refers to the PFD strength, not personal protection.

CARE AND STORAGE OF PFDS

Twice during the boating season, give your PFDs a visual inspection, because the protection and buoyancy a PFD provides will decrease as it ages. Check to see that the straps and hardware are not frayed or cut and that the buoyancy material hasn't hardened or gotten lumpy. If so, replace it with a new one.

Don't use a PFD of any kind as a backrest, kneeling pad, or fender board. Store it in an accessible compartment with good ventilation.

VISUAL DISTRESS SIGNALS

All boats are required to carry some sort of visual distress signals when operating in coastal waters, the Great Lakes, territorial seas, and those water connected directly to them, up to a point where a body of water is less than 2 miles wide. They include pyrotechnic and nonpyrotechnic devices, which should be in serviceable condition and readily accessible. A boat owner should have three signals for day use and three signals for night use. Some meet both day and night use requirements. They are marked with a date showing the service life, which must not have expired.

Distress signals have pros and cons, because no single device is ideal under all conditions. Pyrotechnics are highly visible signals, but there is a potential for injury, because they produce a hot flame, and the residue can cause burns, damaging a boat or other property. Pistol and hand-held parachute flares and meteors are not too unlike firearms and are therefore considered dangerous.

Pyrotechnic signals include:
- Hand-held or aerial red pyrotechnic red flares
- Hand-held or floating pyrotechnic orange smoke
- Launchers for aerial red meteors or parachute flares

Nonpyrotechnic signals include:
- Orange distress flag
- Electric distress light

On the next page are examples of the variety and combinations of devices which can be carried in order to meet the requirements.

- Three hand-held red flares (day and night)
- One hand-held red flare and two parachute flares (day and night)
- One hand-held orange smoke signal, two floating orange smoke signals (day), and one electric distress light (night only)

SOUND-PRODUCING DEVICES

Boats under 12 meters (39.4 feet) are required to carry a whistle, horn, or bell for meeting, crossing, and overtaking situations with another boat. A sound signal is also needed during periods of fog with restricted visibility to signal other boats of your whereabouts.

FIRE EXTINGUISHERS

Fire-fighting devices approved by the U.S. Coast Guard are required on certain boats. Extinguishers are categorized by a letter and a symbol—for example, B-I. The letter indicates the type of fire the unit is designed to extinguish. Type B extinguishers are for putting out fires caused by flammable liquids, such as gasoline, oil, and grease fires. The number after the letter indicates the relative capacity of the extinguisher. The higher the number, the more fire-fighting agent the extinguisher contains and the longer it can fight a fire. The weight of the extinguisher is directly proportional to its fire-fighting capacity; checking the weight is also the only reliable method to see if some types of extinguishers have a full charge.

If any one or more of the following conditions exist, fire extinguishers are required:

- There is an inboard engine.
- There are closed compartments and compartments under seats where portable fuel tanks may be stored.
- There are double bottoms not sealed to the hull or not completely filled with flotation material.
- There is a closed living space.
- There are closed stowage compartments in which combustible or flammable materials are stored.
- There is a permanently installed fuel tank or tanks.

If you are required to have a fire extinguisher aboard, you need at least one portable B-I type on a boat that is less than 26 feet long, and at least two B-Is or one B-II if it is over 26 feet but less than 40 feet.

Periodically check fire extinguishers to see that the seals and tamper indicators are not broken or missing. Look at the operating range and see that pressure gauges or indicators are in the correct range. Notice whether the unit appears to have any physical damage, such as corrosion, leakage, or a clogged nozzle. If there are signs of damage, remove it and take it to a fire extinguisher company that services units.

Coast Guard–approved extinguishers are hand-operated and portable, either B-I or B-II classification, and have a specific marine-type mounting bracket. When installing the mounting bracket, make sure that it is conveniently located and easy to reach from where a possible fire might occur, such as near the engine and galley.

To operate an extinguisher, remember the word PASS to guide you through the sequence:

Pull the pin, or on some units release a lock latch by pressing a puncture lever.

Aim the nozzle or its horn or hose at the base of the fire holding it upright.

Squeeze or press the handle to release the extinguishing agent.

Sweep from side to side at the base of the fire, or use short bursts aimed at the base.

Always check for smoldering embers to make sure the fire doesn't flash back or start up again.

VENTILATION

The ventilation system on a boat that exhausts fumes should be in good working condition. Make sure all openings are free of obstructions, ducts are not blocked or torn, blowers are operating properly, and worn-out components are replaced with equivalent marine-type equipment.

Gasoline vapors can explode. Before starting a gasoline engine, operate the blower for at least four minutes and check the engine compartment bilge for gasoline vapors.

All boats built after April 25, 1940, that use gasoline for electrical generation or mechanical power or propulsion must have a ventilation system.

A natural ventilation system consists of at least two ventilator ducts, fitted with cowls or their equivalent: a minimum of one exhaust duct installed so as to extend from the open atmosphere to

A ventilation system is required to remove explosive or flammable gases and vapors.

the lower portion of the bilge; and a minimum of one intake duct installed so as to extend to a point at least midway to the bilge or at least below the level of the carburetor air intake.

A powered ventilation system consists of one or more exhaust blowers. Each intake duct for an exhaust blower should be in the lower one-third of the compartment and above the normal accumulation of bilge water.

If your boat was built between April 25, 1940, and July 31, 1978, a natural ventilation system is required for all engine and fuel tank compartments, and other spaces to which explosive or flammable gases and vapors for these compartments may flow, except compartments that are open to the atmosphere.

Boats built after 1980 have to comply with the Coast Guard Ventilation Standard, a manufacturer requirement.

BACKFIRE FLAME CONTROL

All boats with a gasoline engine installed after April 25, 1940, except outboard motors, must be equipped with an acceptable means of backfire flame control, such as a flame arrester. It must be suitably attached to the air intake with a flame-tight connection.

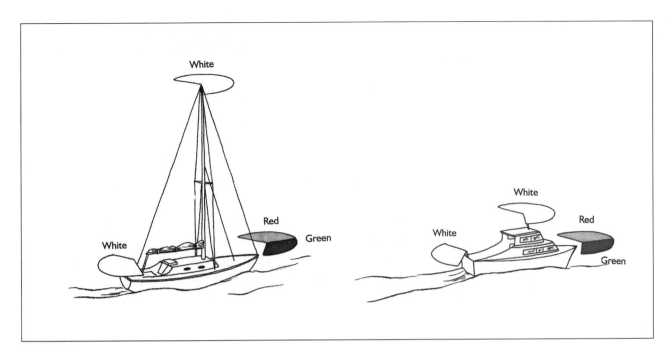

NAVIGATION LIGHTS

All recreational boats are required to display navigational lights between sunset and sunrise and other periods of reduced visibility, such as fog, heavy rain, and haze.

Power-driven boats must exhibit a masthead light forward and aft of the centerline of the boat, sidelights, and a stern light. Boats under sail and power must exhibit lights as if they were powerboats with forward light.

All boats under 65 feet under power must display a white masthead light, red and green sidelights, and a white stern light.

Sailboats less than 65 feet not under power must display red and green sidelights and a white stern light. The sidelights and stern light can be combined into a single masthead mounted light.

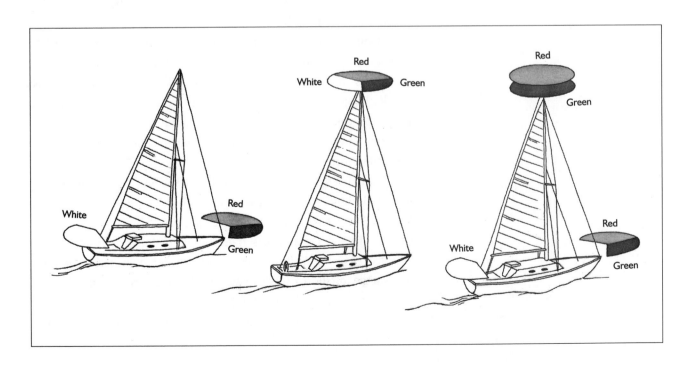

A SHIP STATION LICENSE

All operators of VHF radios are required to have a ship station license. VHF stands for "very high frequency." The fixed-mount radios provide two-way marine communications with a range of 5 to 25 miles. They are the most important safety equipment aboard a boat, because they are the fastest and most direct link to the Coast Guard and emergency services such as towing, marinas, and mechanics.

The license costs $35 for five years and is issued by the Marine Ship Service of the Federal Communications Commission. If you have plans to purchase additional equipment such as radar in the future, include that on the application. Otherwise you have to pay an additional $35 for each new application.

You'll be assigned a call sign, which must be posted on or near the radio.

If used as the primary radio, a hand-held VHF, which is less powerful than a fixed-mount unit, does not require a license, because it is considered a backup to the fixed-mount unit.

For an application contact: Marine Ship Service, FCC, P.O. Box 358275, Pittsburgh, PA 15251-5275. Ask for Form 506.

POLLUTION REGULATIONS

The discharge or depositing of any refuse matter (including trash, garbage, and oil and other liquid pollutants) into the waters of the United States is prohibited.

Boats 26 feet or longer must display a durable placard at least 4 by 9 inches in a prominent location notifying crew and passengers of the discharge restriction. The placard warns against the discharge of plastic and other forms of garbage within the navigable waters of the United States and specifies discharge restrictions beyond the territorial sea, which generally ends 3 nautical miles from the seashore.

Boats used exclusively in the Great Lakes may use the placard described above or one that reads: "The discharge of ALL garbage into the Great Lakes or their connecting or tributary waters is prohibited." In the Great Lakes it is illegal to dump anything except fresh fish, fish parts, dishwater, or gray water anywhere regardless of distance offshore. (Gray water is drainage from a dishwasher, shower, laundry, bath, or washbasin.)

Boats 26 feet and longer must display a durable placard at

least 5 by 8 inches fixed in a conspicuous place in the machinery spaces or at the bilge pump control station citing that the discharge of oil is prohibited with a penalty of $5,000.

MARINE SANITATION DEVICE

Recreational boats are not required to be equipped with a toilet. However, the Clean Water Act requires that if a toilet is installed on a recreational boat it should be equipped with an operable Marine Sanitation Device, or MSD, that is certified by the Coast Guard. The most stringent rules apply in "no-discharge areas," where pump-out facilities are used. Installed toilets that are not equipped with an MSD and that discharge raw sewage directly over the side are illegal.

Recreational boats under 65 feet long may install a Type I, II, or III Marine Sanitation Device.

- Type I is certified to treat the sewage with disinfectant chemicals, and by other means, before it is discharged into the water. The treated discharge must meet certain health standards for bacteria content and must not show any visible floating solids.
- Type II is certified to provide a higher level of sewage treatment. It is larger and requires more power than a Type I device, so it's often used in larger boats.
- Type III includes recirculating and incinerating MSDs and holding tanks. It does not allow the discharge of sewage. Holding tanks, probably the most common type of Type III MSD, store sewage until it can be pumped out to a reception facility or "pump-out station" on shore or at sea beyond the territorial waters of the United States.

Portable toilets are not considered installed toilets, so they are not subject to the MSD regulations. But they are subject to disposal regulations, which prohibit the disposal of raw sewage within territorial waters (within a 3-mile limit), in the Great Lakes, or in navigable rivers.

A No Discharge Zone is an area of water requiring greater environmental protection and where even the discharge of treated sewage could be harmful. When operating in a No Discharge Zone, a Type I or Type II MSD must be secured in some way to prevent discharge. Closing the seacock and padlocking, using a nonreleasable wire tie, or removing the seacock handle would be sufficient. Locking the door to the head with a padlock or a door handle key lock is another acceptable method of securing the MSD while in a No Discharge Zone.

In general, all freshwater lakes, similar freshwater reservoirs that have no navigable connection with other bodies or waters, and rivers not capable of interstate vessel traffic are by definition considered No Discharge Zones. States may establish No Discharge Zones with Environmental Protection Agency approval, and many have done so. Check with your local boating law authority for more information or call the Coast Guard Hotline at 1 (800) 368-5647.

COURTESY MARINE EXAMINATION

A Courtesy Marine Examination, also known as CME, is a free service conducted by the Coast Guard Auxiliary to promote safe boating. It is a courtesy inspection of your boat's condition and safety equipment. The boat owner receives a CME Decal or Seal of Safety when the boat meets the requirements. The CME requirements are parallel to and sometimes exceed the federal requirements.

The Auxiliary CME Decal indicates that the following items have passed inspection:

- Alternate means of propulsion. Boats under 16 feet must carry a paddle or oars; if it's an outboard it should have a separate fuel tank and starting source other than the main motor.
- Anchoring. A boat must be equipped with an anchor and line of suitable size and length for the waters in which it is operated.
- Dewatering device. All boats must carry at least one effective manual device (portable bilge pump, bucket, scoop, etc.) for bailing water, in addition to any installed electrical bilge pump.
- Fuel system. Portable fuel tanks (7 gallons or less) must be constructed of sturdy material and be in good condition, free of excessive corrosion. They should be secured and have vents, a vapor-tight leakproof cap, and no leaks. Permanent tanks should be free of corrosion and not leak. The tanks should be vented to the outside of the hull, and the fill pipe and plate must fit tightly and be located outside of closed compartments.
- Galley and heating equipment. Appliances and their fuel tanks must be properly secured, and the system must not leak. There should be no flammable material in the vicinity of the stoves or heaters. And only common appliance fuels must be used, not gasoline, naphtha, or benzene. The shutoff valves must be readily accessible, and there should be adequate ventilation for the appliances and their fuel supply.

- Electrical systems. Wiring must be in good condition and properly installed with no exposed areas or deteriorated insulation. The system must be protected by fuses or manual-resetting circuit breakers. The switches and fuse panel must be protected from rain or spray. Batteries must be secured to prevent movement and the terminals covered to prevent accidental arcing.
- State requirements. Additional safety equipment required by the state where the CME is conducted must be on the boat.

EMERGENCY SITUATIONS

Murphy's Law often rules when there's an emergency on board. Conditions are usually chaotic. To avoid weather-related emergencies, check the latest weather forecast for your boating area. If weather warnings are in effect, don't go out unless you're confident your boat can be navigated safely. Don't go out when there is a coppery haze and building cumulus clouds signaling a thunderstorm, which can have lightning ahead of or behind it. Make sure your boat is well equipped for an emergency, with a sturdy anchor and line, paddle or oars in case the engine stops or your sail rig fails, and of course, the required distress signals.

FIRE

Everyone on board a boat should be familiar with how to operate the fire extinguisher and where it is located. If a fire occurs, direct your passengers to put on their life jackets. Have one person operate the extinguisher while another radios for help or puts out a distress signal. If the fire is in the motor or stove, shut off the fuel supply immediately. Try to contain the fire if it is in a cabinet or hatch by closing it off.

Stop or slow the speed of the boat so the wind doesn't increase the fire's strength. Turn the boat downwind if the fire is in the forward area of the boat to lessen the wind's effect on the fire. If the fire is in the stern area of the boat, steer the boat into the wind. If the item burning is easy to remove, such as a bunk cushion, throw it overboard. Disconnect all sources of electrical power on the boat. Also, if possible, remove any flammable materials such as cushions and portable fuel tanks if they are in the path of the fire.

Have adequate and readily accessible extinguishers near the galley and engine compartment where a fire might occur.

MAN OVERBOARD

When a passenger falls overboard, immediately throw anything buoyant, such as a PFD or a Type IV cushion, to mark his location and give him something to hold on to. Stop the boat and reverse course and return to the swimmer as quickly as possible. Have someone on board spot the swimmer and keep him in sight while the skipper turns the boat around. Be careful to approach the swimmer from the downwind side so the boat can't drift down onto the person in the water. Approach the swimmer on the helm side so the skipper has an unimpaired view of the swimmer. Lower a ladder and throw a line attached to a PFD or a cushion for the swimmer to grab.

If the swimmer needs help in getting aboard, another crew member can assist him, but make sure anyone who goes in the water is wearing a PFD with a line attached to the boat. If there's no ladder available, turn off the engine or outboard and use it as a step to get into the boat.

GROUNDING

Going aground can be more harmful to your pride than your hull, especially if the bottom is a nice soft sandy one. Turn off the engine and lift or tilt the drive unit of your motor or outboard.

The challenge comes if you are in tidal waters and you go aground while the tide is going out, because you'll have several hours to wait for the tide to return and raise the water level. On a rising tide, a grounding can mean simply waiting for the tide to roll in and lift the hull so it floats freely.

If you go aground in nontidal waters that are shallow, you can often jump overboard and push or rock the hull back and forth to break it loose from the bottom.

With a strong current or wind conditions blowing you onto the shore, use an anchor to kedge off, or pull the boat in the opposite direction. If conditions permit, swim an anchor line out with the anchor floated on a cushion or in a cooler, however you can maneuver it. Take it out far enough to hold the boat so it's not washed onto the shore into even shallower water.

If you're on a sailboat, you can use the force of the wind in the mainsail to help you float the boat by swinging the boom to the downwind side of the boat. The boat will heave to one side and possibly it will be enough to dislodge the keel from the bottom.

When the boat is floating free, check for damage to the hull. Look for leaks in the hull or damage to the propeller.

The wake from another boat might be enough to loosen the grip of the bottom on the hull, so if you see boats nearby you can ask them to create a wake.

To take a tow from another boater who offers to try to pull your boat off, be careful to fasten the line to a secure cleat and stand clear in case the line breaks under the strain of the tow.

Another option is to use the VHF to call for a private tow service. Such services usually monitor the VHF. Be prepared to give your location, and ask what the charge is for the service.

COLLISION

A collision with another boat or with a fixed or floating object usually happens quickly. It can result in a minor scraping of the hull or trim or major damage to the integrity of the hull. When a collision occurs, check that the passengers are not injured and look for leaks in the hull. A hole above the waterline and damage to the topsides are a concern, but especially look below in the engine compartment and bilge area for leaking water.

If you are taking on water, turn on the bilge pump and use buckets and sponges or rags to soak up the water. Stop the leak temporarily by stuffing the hole with any packing material at hand. Use rags, towels, blankets, pillows, sails, whatever is available. Have a crew member stand by the leak, and maintain pressure until you have safely returned to a marina where you can be hauled or to your launch ramp.

RULES OF THE ROAD

G etting from point A to point B on a boat has fewer restrictions than driving a car from one destination to another, because instead of defined roads and pattern traffics, there's open water. But there's a well-thought-out system designed for the safe passage of recreational boats and commercial craft.

INLAND RULES

The right-of-way of boats or "who goes first" in various situations is set down by rules to prevent collisions. Just as traffic lights regulate the movement of cars, trucks, and buses traveling at various speeds and various directions, navigation rules were devised to prevent recreational and commercial boats, ships, and barges from colliding with one another.

The rules are divided into two parts: Inland and International. Inland Rules cover most of the coastal waters, lakes, rivers, and waterways in the United States. International Rules deal with vessels offshore, but include some U.S. coastal areas. If you look on a navigational chart you'll see there are purple dashed demarcation lines.

▲ ▲ ▲
AVOIDING A COLLISION COURSE

Sometimes it is difficult to discern if you should change course to avoid a collision when you see an approaching boat on your starboard side. For a quick check, eyeball the angle between the two boats. If the angle seems to increase as the boats get closer (the boat moves toward your stern), you'll probably pass ahead of the other boat. If the angle appears to be getting smaller (the boat is moving toward your bow) you will probably pass behind the boat. But if the angle remains the same, you're on a collision course and should take evasive action to pass its stern.

▼ ▼ ▼

The Inland Rules are discussed here because they apply in most U.S. boating waters. They refer to boats being either "privileged" (the "stand-on vessel") or "burdened" (the "give-way vessel"). When privileged, a boat has the right-of-way and should maintain its speed and course. A burdened boat should steer clear of the privileged boat and give it the right-of-way.

In any situation you may want to use your VHF radio to communicate with another boat so both you and the other skipper know who is going to do what.

BOW TO BOW

If two boats under power meet head on, each of them should take action and turn to starboard. By doing so, they pass each other on their port sides.

When two powerboats are passing starboard to starboard, one of the boats should signal its intent with two short horn blasts, and the other should acknowledge it by sounding two short blasts.

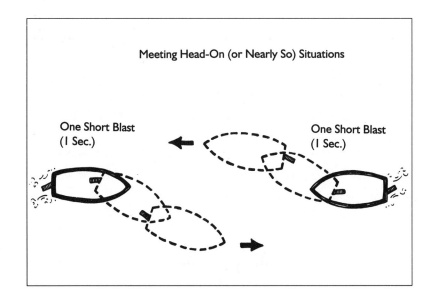

Meeting Head-On (or Nearly So) Situations

One Short Blast (1 Sec.)

One Short Blast (1 Sec.)

When two boats under power meet head on, each of them should turn to starboard so they pass each other port side to port side.

CROSSING AT AN ANGLE

When two boats under power are approaching each other at an angle, there is a potential for a collision because at some point their view of each other will be limited, just as there is a blind spot when you're driving a car.

A boat approaching dead ahead to a point 22.5 degrees behind your beam on your port is referred to as being in the danger zone.

When two boats under power cross each other's paths at an angle, the boat with the approaching boat on its starboard side must give way and pass astern. When changing course, make it obvious what you are doing.

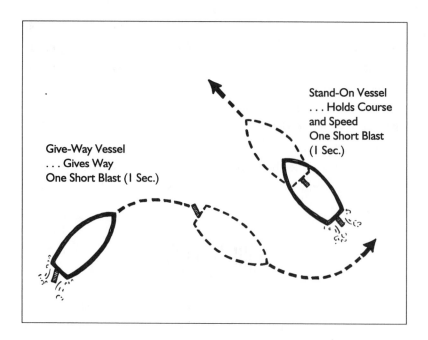

Give-Way Vessel
. . . Gives Way
One Short Blast (1 Sec.)

Stand-On Vessel
. . . Holds Course
and Speed
One Short Blast
(1 Sec.)

The reason is that you have the right-of-way and the other vessel should give way, but it's up to you to be certain that this happens. You should hold your course and speed, but if the other vessel does not appear to alter course or speed to avoid a collision, you must. In almost every case it will be safer for you to alter course to starboard. If you decide that you must change course to avoid the other boat, make your course and speed change a large one so the other boat will see exactly what you are doing.

If a boat is approaching from your starboard side, it is in the give-way zone and you are the burdened or give-way vessel, so you must alter your course to starboard to pass on the other boat's port side or behind the boat if it is crossing your bow. Here again, make your course or speed correction large enough so that your intentions are clear to the other skipper.

OVERTAKING

When you approach another boat from either port or starboard from more than 22.5 degrees abaft or behind its beam, you are said to be overtaking it. In both these situations you must give way and keep clear of the other boat.

When two boats under power are running in the same direction and one approaches from behind to pass and overtake the other, the skipper of the passing boat is the give-way vessel and must continue on a safe course, keeping clear of the boat he is passing. Approaching from the starboard side, the horn signal is one short blast; from the port, the horn signal is two short blasts.

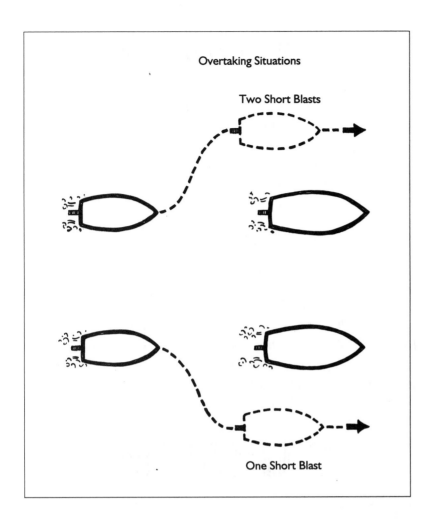

The boat approaching from astern must stay clear of the boat ahead. If passing to starboard, signal one short horn blast; to port, signal two short blasts. The boat ahead will answer with the same horn signal if passing is safe.

If conditions are safe and there is no obstruction ahead, the boat being passed should acknowledge the situation and reply with the same number of horn blasts. When such action isn't safe, the boat being passed should alert the passing boat to a dangerous situation ahead by sounding five or more short blasts. Use this horn signal whenever the situation could develop into eminent danger.

A skipper approaching another boat at an angle should steer to the stern of the boat or alter course to starboard if no other boat is approaching from that direction. If that is the case, the approaching boat should reduce speed or change course to port.

LEAVING THE DOCK OR CROSSING A CHANNEL

If you are crossing a river at right angles or have just pulled into a channel, these rules are changed and call for keeping clear of upriver or downriver traffic.

When leaving a dock, a ferry boat has the right-of-way over other boats, but all other boats leaving a dock should give way to boats in the channel or waterway.

NARROW WINDING CHANNEL

You can't always see approaching boats around a bend until they're "in your face," so signal a horn warning of one long blast. The approaching boat should respond with the same signal so both skippers know they have communicated. Both boats should keep to their starboard side of the channel as they pass each other, paying heed to their respective shorelines.

UNDER SAIL

When two sailboats are under sail and are on different points of sail, the boat on the starboard tack has the right-of-way. (The boat with wind blowing on the starboard side is on a starboard tack, with its sails set on the portside of the boat. The sailboat on a port tack has wind on its port side and the sail set on its starboard side.)

WINDWARD BOAT KEEP CLEAR

If two sailboats are under sail alone and head on, they are both on the same tack, because the wind is coming from the same side. One

When two sailboats are passing, the windward boat should keep clear of the leeward boat on the same tack by steering for its stern.

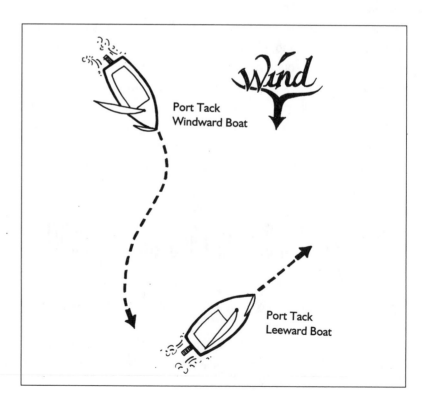

Port Tack
Windward Boat

Port Tack
Leeward Boat

of them will be windward of or farther upwind than the other. The other boat is leeward and has the right-of-way, because it may be restricted and blocked by the wind so it has less maneuverability. The windward boat must give way to the leeward boat in that situation.

BOAT UNDER SAIL HAS RIGHT-OF-WAY

If a sailboat is under sail and meets a powerboat or sailboat under power, the sailboat generally has the right-of-way. The boat under power has to keep clear of the sailboat. The exceptions are when the sailboat is overtaking a powerboat—then the general overtaking rule applies. And a sailboat encountering a commercial fishing boat, such as a shrimp boat with nets down, must give it the right-of-way, because the boat is restricted in its maneuverability.

MIGHT MAKES RIGHT

This rule applies to all situations involving recreational boats and ships, because large vessels do not have the maneuverability or ability to stop quickly and are consequently considered privileged. Common sense dictates that when possible, recreational boats should steer clear of large vessels.

12

NAVIGATION

The science of navigation has been practiced for centuries. There are volumes written on this topic, but most texts deal with techniques that are more suited to navigating a supertanker than a 30-foot cruiser.

On most small boats there is hardly room to unroll a chart, let alone place it on a dedicated chart table. This does not lessen the need for you to keep track of your position—it just calls for a slightly different technique. In this section you will learn basic navigation skills that will enable you to navigate your boat with confidence.

Of course, there are complete books dedicated to the science of navigation. If you plan an extensive cruise or long to venture far offshore, further study is strongly recommended. Probably the most intriguing aspect of navigation is that there is always something new to learn.

NAVIGATION KNOW-HOW

In order to get a driver's license you have to pass a test. You are questioned on the basic traffic rules, and you can miss a few of them, but you have to identify all the street signs. Most people don't have to take a test to operate a boat, but it is just as important to know the nautical street signs.

The street signs you find on the water are called aids to navigation. Just like street signs and traffic lights, aids to navigations have many different functions and take on different forms.

NAUTICAL CHARTS

A chart or nautical map is an aid with information about a body of water. Since the collection of such data is a monumental job, it's done by the National Oceanic and Atmospheric Administration (NOAA), a government agency. These charts are accurate scale maps and are published in four basic scales:

- Harbor charts: 1:50,000 scale or larger. These show great detail.
- Coast charts: 1:50,000 to 1:150,000 scale. These are used to navigate the coastal waters and enter rivers and bays from the ocean.
- General charts: 1:150,000 to 1:600,000 scale. These don't show much landmass detail and are used to navigate well offshore between distant ports.
- Sailing charts: smaller than 1:600,000 scale. These are used for long voyages at sea.

Harbor charts and coast charts are the ones most useful to the small boater. The larger the scale (remember that 1:50,000 is a larger fraction than 1:150,000), the more detail. Some harbor and coastal charts are available in a small craft folio format.

The amount of effort to keep charts up to date is reflected in their price, which has risen steadily. To help offset the high cost of charts, publishing companies have collected related government charts, reproduced them, and published bound volumes. These chart volumes cover large areas and are less expensive than an array of individual charts. They are also very convenient, since the book of charts takes up a lot less room than individual charts and is easier to handle. Consider purchasing one of these publications if you plan to cruise away from your local waters and need more than a couple of government charts.

The amount of information on a typical chart is astounding. You can spend hours looking over a new chart and still discover some area or building that you hadn't noticed. This abundance of information can also make charts a bit intimidating or confusing. A quick tour of a typical chart should set you straight and take most of the mystery out of reading it.

THE LEGEND

At the top or at some other conspicuous location on the chart is the legend. This area contains the name of the chart and other important information, such as the scale of the chart and what the units of measurement for depth are. Large-scale charts usually have the depth soundings expressed in feet, but smaller-scale charts may use fathoms, so this is vital information to read before you begin using the chart.

The title block and legend of a nautical chart contain the name of the chart, its scale, the unit of measurement for water depth, and other information.

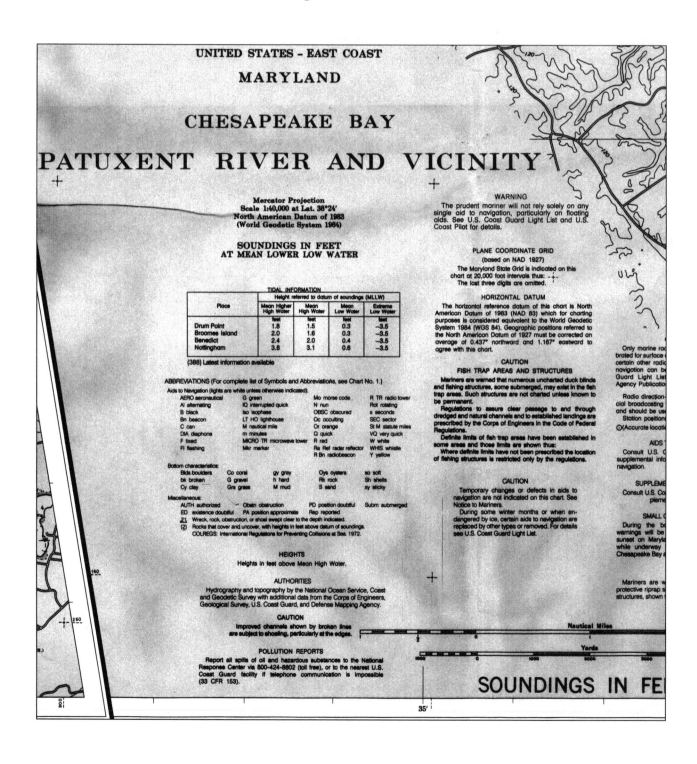

This area also contains tidal information, giving the mean high and low tidal ranges for the charted area. Sounding information or the depth of the water is usually expressed at mean low tide, and the height of bridges and structures is usually given at mean high tide. In some locations the difference between high and low tide can be 10 to 15 feet or more, so this information is important to know when using the chart.

In addition to tide and sounding information contained in the legend, the chart has the latitude marked on the right and left edge and the longitude on the top and bottom edge. Aids to navigation are explained and located on the chart, with different symbols for exact and approximate locations. At least one distance scale and compass rose is located on the chart to help you plan and plot a course on the chart.

At the bottom left corner of the chart the NOAA number and publication date are stated. This date is important, because markers and aids can change by being moved or renumbered, and unless you're using an up-to-date chart, navigating can be confusing. You can keep your charts updated by getting the Notice to Mariners published by the Coast Guard and making the revisions and corrections on your chart.

SOUNDINGS

Understanding a nautical chart is not difficult, since the chartmaker has tried to make it as easy to understand as possible. At first glance the hundreds of soundings printed on the chart are probably its most notable feature.

The actual soundings printed on the chart are usually adjusted to represent the water depth at mean low water. This means that the water is usually deeper than charted unless there is an unusually low or minus tide. Tide tables are published by NOAA, and there are publications like *Reed's Nautical Almanac* and the *Coast Pilot*, which gives the time of high and low tide and the height of the tide for just about every tidal area in the country. You can also find this information in your local newspaper.

If you study the sounding you will see that in many areas, soundings of the same depth are connected with lines. These lines help display the bottom contour. Contour lines that are far apart represent gradual changes in the bottom depth, while contour lines close together show steep changes. This information is very useful, since it is important to know whether the bottom will gradually grow shallower as you approach the shore or remain deep and then suddenly shoal with little warning.

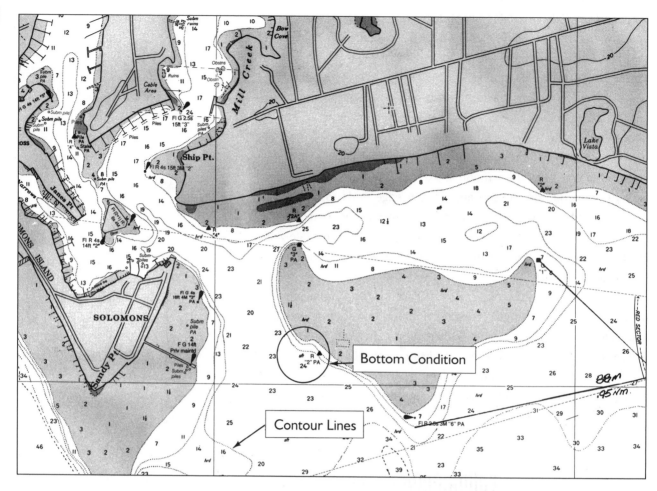

A chart shows information on the water depth, tides, navigational aids, and other features.

RULE OF THUMB ABOUT TIDES

Most tides rise and fall in a six-hour period. During the first few hours after a high or low tide it starts to rise or fall slowly. Then it picks up speed during the third and fourth hours and slows again during the last two hours.

If you don't have a tide table, the Rule of Twelfths can give you a rough estimate of the depth of the water during the six-hour period.

To use this rule, add the number of twelfths corresponding to each hour past the last high or low tide, then multiply the tidal range by the fraction.

For example, four hours after low tide, the tide will have come in about 9/12 (the total of the first through fourth hours) of its total range. If the tide has a range of 4 feet, then it has risen about 3 feet (4 feet × 9/12) and has a foot or so more to rise before the next high tide.

Hour	Hourly Rise or Fall	Total Rise or Fall
1st	1/12 of range	1/12 of range
2nd	2/12 of range	3/12 of range
3rd	3/12 of range	6/12 of range
4th	3/12 of range	9/12 of range
5th	2/12 of range	11/12 of range
6th	1/12 of range	12/12 of range

BOTTOM CONDITIONS

In addition to the water depth, the chart also shows the composition of the bottom. This information is printed between the soundings and is very helpful in selecting an anchorage. A soft bottom (*sft*) will hold an anchor better than a rocky (*rky*) or hard (*hrd*) bottom.

COMPASS ROSE

Maps and charts are drawn so that north is at the top. On road maps this is all you have to know to use the map, since you don't steer your car by a compass but must follow the road. Of course, this is not the case with a boat, so a nautical chart must provide more precise data for using a compass. All nautical charts have a circular 360-degree compass diagram printed on them, often in several places. Such a diagram is called a compass rose. The outer ring of the compass rose is aligned with true north on the chart. The outer ring is in exact alignment with the latitude and longitude lines on the chart, which run north and south and east and west.

The outer ring of the compass rose is aligned with true north on the chart and the inner ring is offset to the east or west from true north to indicate magnetic north on the chart.

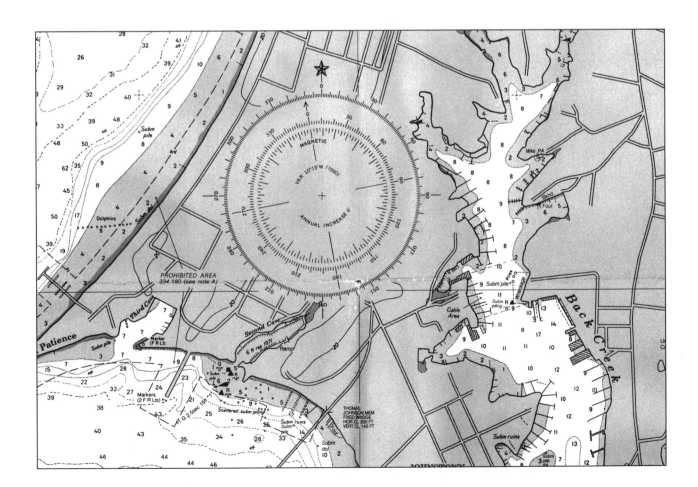

The magnetic pole of the earth is not exactly aligned with the geographic pole, so the inner compass ring is offset to the east or west from true north to indicate magnetic north on the chart. Since you steer your boat with the compass, it is the inner ring that you should use to determine your compass course.

Each chart has its own compass rose, and it should be used, since the variation between true north and magnetic north will change as you sail from one area to another. If you do most of your boating close to your home port, then the variation will be very slight. If you look at the compass rose you will see that West variation is added to the true course and East variation is subtracted. This is done graphically by the compass rose.

AIDS TO NAVIGATION

To help you find your way on the chart and avoid dangers, the chart indicates the location of aids to navigation such as lighthouses, navigational buoys, and daymarks (discussed below). In addition to this information, the locations of prominent landmarks that are visible from the water such as towers, smokestacks, church steeples, and other buildings are printed on the chart. Depending on where you are located or plan to cruise, you may encounter several different systems of aids to navigation.

MARKERS AND BUOYS

The location of the boating waters you're in determines how the waterways are marked with a buoy system. If you boat or cruise along either the Atlantic or Pacific coast or on the Great Lakes, you will be aided by U.S. Aids to Navigation. This uniform system uses numbered red, black, or green lighted and unlighted aids to navigation. These buoys and lights follow the general rule of Red, Right, Returning. That is, keep the red markers to your right as you return from the sea or enter the body of water. The general rule follows a clockwise pattern around the U.S. coast from Maine on the Atlantic to the state of Washington on the Pacific.

To help you identify each aid, it is not only numbered and colored but also has a distinctive shape. Although there may be slight variations in some of the aids, especially lighthouses and other structures, most aids to navigation in the U.S. system have these characteristics.

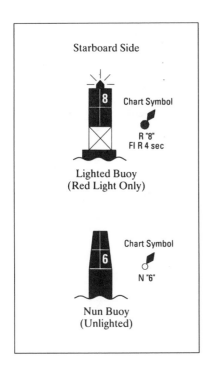

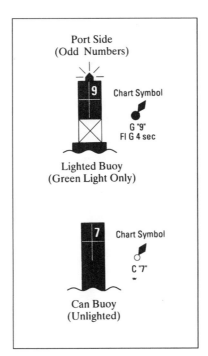

Far left: Nun buoys are cone-topped even-numbered red buoys that you pass to starboard when returning to port from the open water.

Left: Can buoys are flat-topped odd-numbered black or green buoys that you keep to port when returning to a harbor or entering a river or channel.

- Nun buoy. Cone-topped even-numbered red buoy. Generally a nun should be kept to the right or starboard when returning to a harbor or entering a river or channel. In most situations you should not pass between a nun and the shore.
- Can buoy. Flat-topped odd-numbered black or green buoy. Generally a can should be kept to the left or port when returning to a harbor or entering a river or channel. As with nuns, in most situations you should not pass between a can and the shore.
- Mid-channel marker. Either a can buoy or a nun buoy can be used as a mid-channel marker. You can pass on either side of these aids. They are identified on the chart with letters instead

▲ ▲ ▲

READING RANGES

When you're steering your boat between two aids to navigation and there is a crosscurrent that may set your boat off course, always look behind as well as ahead. By looking back to check the location of the aid you just passed you can tell if your boat is being set by the current. As long as the aid you passed is aligned with your stern you know you are on a straight line between the aids. If you steer for the aid off the bow only, your boat will appear to be heading toward it even though it is being set by the current.

On longer stretches between aids where the marker you pass may be out of sight, check your compass course as you pass the first aid. Then check your heading as you steer toward the next mark. If you are steering toward the mark and the compass course is changing, then you are being set by the current. Steer high or low of the course to compensate.

▼ ▼ ▼

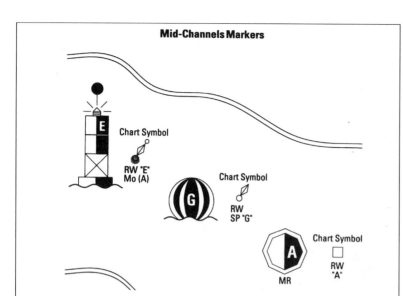

Mid-Channels Markers

Chart Symbol
RW "E"
Mo (A)

Chart Symbol
RW
SP "G"

Chart Symbol
RW
"A"
MR

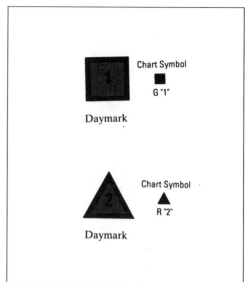

Chart Symbol
G "1"
Daymark

Chart Symbol
R "2"
Daymark

Above: Nun or can buoys can be used as mid-channel markers and are usually striped vertically or horizontally.

Above right: Daymarks are square odd-numbered black or green shapes on the port side of the channel or red triangular even-numbered shapes on the starboard side of the channel.

of numbers. Mid-channel markers can be vertically or horizontally striped depending on whether they are at a junction. Generally mid-channel nun buoys signify that the preferred channel is to port and can buoys tell you that the preferred channel is to starboard.

• Daymark. In shallow water and along many channels, daymarks are used instead of buoys. These are usually numbered triangular or square markers placed on posts. Red triangular even-numbered daymarks are the same as nuns, and square black or green odd-numbered daymarks are the same as cans.

LIGHTED AIDS

All of these aids to navigation can be lighted. Cans can have white or green lights and nuns have white or red lights. Lighthouses and other large aids to navigation generally have white lights. Some lighthouses have lights that show a colored light, usually red, when viewed from certain angles. This alerts navigators that they are approaching from a dangerous angle and that there is some obstruction between the light and the boat. These red sectors are indicated on the chart.

All lighted aids to navigation have either a fixed nonflashing light or one that flashes at regular intervals. Bridges are marked with red lights to show the drawbridge is closed and with green lights to show it is open. Just as a green traffic light signals "go," green lights mark the centerline of a channel through a fixed bridge. The type of light and its flash pattern are listed in the NOAA publication called the Light List.

SOUND-EMITTING AIDS

All aids can be equipped with an audible sound such as a bell, whistle, or gong so they can be located in limited visibility. Often important aids have both lights and audible sound.

UNIFORM STATE WATERWAY MARKING SYSTEM

On bodies of water within a single state that are not connected to the sea, you'll find state-maintained navigation aids that follow the Uniform State Waterway Marking System. In general, it varies from the U.S. system by using black, not green, markers. A white buoy with a red top marks an obstruction that should be passed to the south or west; a white buoy with a black top marks an obstruction that should be passed to the north or east. A red-and-white vertically striped buoy marks an obstruction that is between the buoy and the nearest shoreline.

OTHER SYSTEMS

If you're on the Intracoastal Waterway, also called the ICW, which runs from New Jersey to Mexico around the tip of Florida, you'll find portions of it have yellow markers along with the red-and-black or red-and-green markers.

Boaters on the Mississippi River and its tributaries above Baton Rouge, Louisiana, and several other rivers that flow toward the Gulf of Mexico follow the Western Rivers System. The aids to navigation are not numbered as in the U.S. system; instead, some have the mileage from a fixed point such as the river entrance.

PRIVATE MARKS

Whenever you can, avoid fishing markers. These markers vary depending on your location. In New England, for example, you'll find lobster pot markers scattered throughout the waters. Steer clear of them, because they are attached to a long line leading to a trap on the bottom. This line can get tangled around your propeller or hung up on your keel or rudder. Pass on the down-current side of the marker to avoid the anchor line, which runs off at an angle upstream toward the trap.

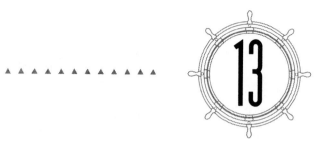

COASTAL PILOTING

Navigating a boat from one destination to another within sight of land is called piloting. As a coastal pilot you have many aids to navigation to call on to help, but there are many more obstructions to avoid. In many of the country's popular boating areas there are few hazards, but in others, swift currents, fog, and a rugged shoreline provide a navigational challenge, even to boaters with local knowledge. In any area, the prudent skipper should have a basic grasp of the piloting skills necessary to navigate the boat safely back into safe waters should the need arise.

Understanding the use of the basic tools of piloting and developing the skill to put these tools to accurate use are not that difficult. Laying out a compass course on a nautical chart requires only a pencil and straightedge; steering that course requires a bit of concentration and a steady hand.

BASIC NAVIGATION SKILLS AND TOOLS

Sailors have put to sea and returned for centuries with only rudimentary navigation. The only essential information they needed was the direction and speed of their boat. This information is readily available to most boaters. All boats, except possibly those used on small inland lakes, should have a compass, and today many boats come equipped with a knot meter or other speed-measuring devices.

To give some meaning to the information your compass provides, you need a navigation chart. To use the chart you need a pair of simple dividers and a course protractor or other plotting instrument. If you are planning a more ambitious cruise into new waters, consider purchasing a hand bearing compass.

CHART, COURSE, AND PROTRACTOR

To put all the information printed on a chart to good use, you must be able to plot bearings on it, which traditionally involves using a set of parallel rules. One edge is aligned with both objects you want to know the bearing between, and then the rule is walked over to the compass rose to read the true or magnetic bearing. This can be a bit of a challenge on a small boat that's bouncing around in choppy waters.

A simple 5-inch-square plastic combination protractor and parallel rule, called a Douglas protractor, is easier to use on a small boat and is just as accurate. The Weems-Zweng course protractor is another user-friendly plotter; both tools are used in the same way. Draw a line representing the course you want to steer between two navigation aids on the chart and then place the protractor so its

A protractor or a combination protractor and parallel rule is probably the best plotting tool to use on a small boat.

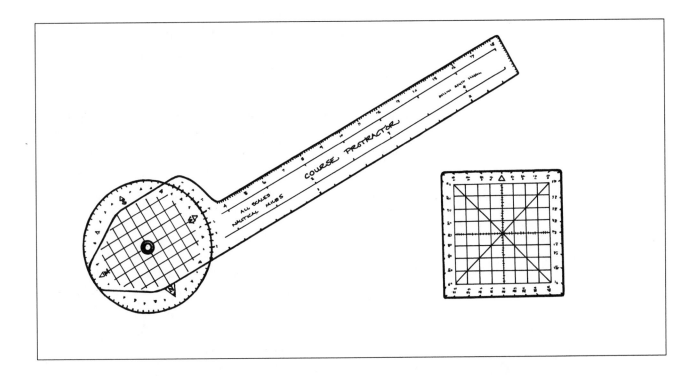

center is over the line. Align the protractor's grid with the latitude or longitude lines on the chart to orient it to true north and then read the true course from the perimeter of the protractor.

For example, using the combination protractor and parallel rule plotter, the true course between the red light "6" off the shoal in front of the Solomons Harbor entrance and light "6A" off Sandy Point is 255 degrees true. This area has about a 10-degree west variation, which must be added to the course to determine the 265-degree magnetic or compass course to steer.

The Weems-Zweng course protractor has a handy variation scale printed on the index area so you can read the magnetic course directly from it. If your compass has any error deviation, it must be added to or subtracted from the magnetic course to get the course you should actually steer on your compass.

COMPASS

The compass is probably the most used and abused navigational instrument ever invented. Luckily the instrument requires little maintenance and, if installed properly, remains fairly accurate throughout its useful life.

Needless to say, your compass should be properly installed and operational if you rely on it for navigation. Assuming that it is functioning properly, it is not difficult to check it out and get a good idea of how accurate it is.

There are whole volumes written on compass adjustment, but most of these techniques are not suitable for use on a small boat. The easiest way to check out a compass is to point your boat at an object and record the compass reading. Then compare that reading to what the chart says the compass heading should be.

For example, on the NOAA chart 12284, a large-scale chart of the Solomons Island harbor area of the Chesapeake Bay, there are several aids to navigation and landmarks that you could use to check out your compass range. A good check for north-south accuracy is the daymark "4" at the entrance and light "3" just south of there. You could also use the end of the pier that is farther south. These aids are in alignment and form a range of 018 degrees to the north and 198 degrees to the south. Remember the area has a 10-degree west variation, so 10 degrees are added to the course plotted on the chart. Another range between the light off Sandy Point "6A" and the light south of the shoal area "6" aligns at 84 and 264 degrees, pretty close to east and west. Apply these principles to a chart of your boating area to compute ranges. Landmarks like chimneys and buildings also make good ranges.

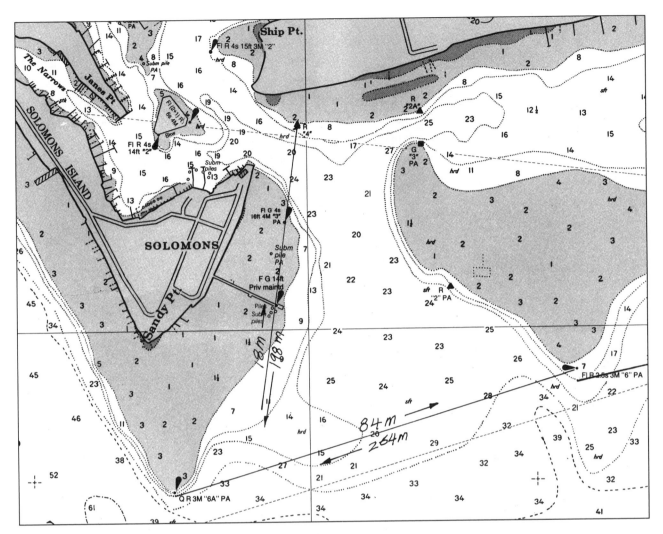

Plot as many ranges as possible in as many directions. On a calm day, carefully steer your boat along these ranges and check your compass readings. If your compass varies from these headings by more than a few degrees, have it professionally adjusted. If the card does not move freely or it has lost a lot of fluid, remove it and have it serviced by a marine navigation equipment dealer.

A couple of degrees one way or another can be tolerated. Write down the compass heading off the chart next to the reading from your compass· on all the headings possible. Use this information to construct a deviation table. If the compass reads less than the charted bearing, then the deviation is east; if more, west.

After you have checked out your compass, you can use this deviation table to correct for these small errors. For example, as we said before, the magnetic bearing between "6A" and "6" is 85 degrees magnetic. Say you carefully steer along the range and find your compass reading is 88 degrees instead of 85. Then you know that on a generally west-to-east heading your compass reads 3 degrees more than it should. In nautical terms, your compass has an easterly deviation of 3 degrees.

To check your compass for deviation, lay out courses between aids to navigation on your chart and then steer these courses and compare your compass reading to that on the chart. The difference is the deviation.

Anytime you want to steer a very accurate compass course around 85 degrees, you must first subtract 3 degrees from the magnetic course to compensate for your compass error. But remember, this 3-degree easterly error is only to be applied when steering close to 85 degrees—your compass may have some other error on another course. That is why you have to run as many ranges as possible to make as complete a deviation table as practical.

If you are planning to cruise outside familar waters and will depend on the compass to navigate over 10 miles between marks, then it is important that your compass be in proper adjustment. For example, if your compass is off by 5 degrees and you steer by it for 5 miles, you will be off course by almost ¹/₂ mile. This could be enough to put you on the rocks.

SPEED/LOG

Knowing how fast you are moving through the water is another key factor in the navigation equation. Steering a compass course for a known amount of time can't in itself be of much use to a navigator, but if the speed is known, the navigator can calculate how far the boat has traveled in a time period and plot it on the chart. Plotting direction and speed on a chart is called dead reckoning.

There are many mechanical and electronic devices available that determine boat speed. Many of these devices also have a log feature that automatically records the distance traveled.

Power boats with a tachometer that measures engine revolutions can also use it as a gauge to determine speed. Calibration of the tachometer can be done by motoring between two known points on the chart at a fixed engine speed and recording the time it takes. Since the time and distance between the aids to navigation or landmarks are taken from the chart, you can calculate the speed by dividing the distance by the time.

For example, in many harbors there is a measured mile painted and marked off on a bulkhead or breakwater that corresponds to one on the chart of the area. You record the time as you pass one of the marks. Let's say it takes you ten minutes to get down to the second mark. If you divide the distance by the time, you will get the speed of your boat ($S = D/T$). Since the formula deals in hours and we have recorded minutes, the formula is modified to $S = 60D/T$. So the boat is moving through the water at 6 knots per hour ($S = (60 \times 1)/10$). If there is any current, run the same course at the same speed in the opposite direction and average the speeds.

Record the calculated speed opposite the engine RPM from the tachometer. Repeat the process at different engine speeds and you

▲ ▲ ▲
CHOOSING BINOCULARS

A good pair of binoculars comes in handy aboard a boat for a variety of situations—identifying a distant mark or buoy, finding the entrance to a harbor, or observing activity aboard another boat. Binoculars use lenses and prisms to magnify distant objects, and they are described by two numbers, such as 7 × 50; 7 is the magnification and 50 is the objective lens diameter. Since binoculars have individual lenses, it's possible to focus each eyepiece independently.

Some binoculars incorporate compasses, which makes them a hand bearing compass of sorts, a handy feature when you're trying to locate something on a distant shore.

For use on a boat look for these features in binoculars: waterproofness, light weight, center focusing, and protective coating.

▼ ▼ ▼

have a table showing the speed of your boat at these engine speeds. This chart will remain accurate as long as you don't drastically change the loading of your boat and keep the bottom and propeller free of marine growth.

HAND BEARING COMPASS

One of the easiest and most accurate methods of finding your location on a chart is to take the compass bearing of an aid to navigation or some other landmark and then plot it on the chart. When a second bearing to a landmark or aid is plotted, the intersection of these lines is your current position, which is called a fix.

Taking a bearing with the main compass is possible by aiming the boat at the aid or landmark and recording the bearing. However, it's a lot more accurate and easier to use a hand bearing compass. Hand bearing compasses come in all different shapes, and some are designed built into binoculars.

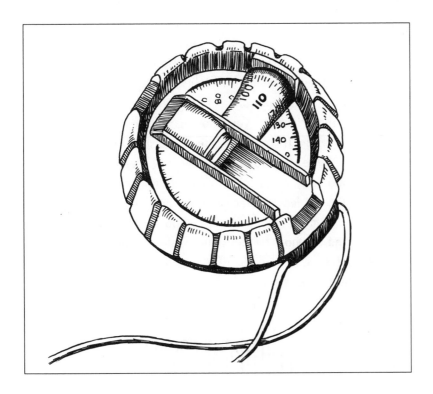

A hand bearing compass is the best tool to use for taking bearings of landmarks and aids to navigation when working out a fix.

DIVIDERS

Nautical charts have distance scales printed on them. A set of dividers allows you to use these scales to measure distances on a nautical chart. Set the points of the dividers to the distance a nau-

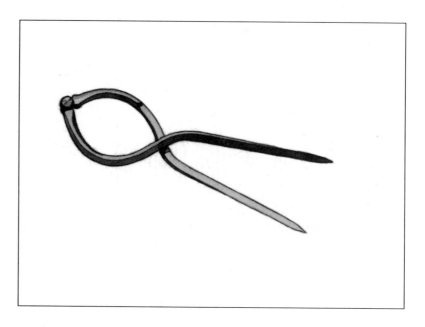

A set of single-handed dividers are handy to use on a boat. They can be used in the closed position to measure distances up to about 8 inches; if needed they can be opened to measure larger distances.

tical mile covers on a particular scale of chart and then use the dividers to measure distances anywhere on the chart.

For example, the distance between the light off Sandy Point and the bridge across the river is 1.1 nautical miles. This is a very large scale chart, so it shows 1 mile and it is a little over 6 inches long. Unless you have large single-hand dividers, this is too far to stretch the dividers, so set the points at the 0 and $\frac{1}{2}$-mile points on the scale. Then move the dividers over to the light off Sandy Point and walk them toward the bridge. It will take two steps to get close to the bridge, so you know it is at least 1 mile between the light and bridge (two $\frac{1}{2}$-mile steps). To measure the short distance between the point of the divider and the bridge, swing the divider around, keeping the point closer to the bridge on the chart. Then close the divider until the other divider point is on the bridge. Go over to the miles scale and place a point of the divider on the zero mark and see how far down the scale the other divider point reaches, in this case about $\frac{1}{10}$ of a mile. The distance between the light and the bridge is then $1\frac{1}{10}$ nautical miles.

PLOTTING A COURSE

Plotting out a day's run on a chart and then following your progress along the chosen path is a lot of fun. If you're cruising to a new destination, it's good information to have, and even when you're in familiar waters it is a good idea to know where you are. Using a chart and the basic tools is not difficult, but like any skill it has to be practiced. The best time to practice plotting is on a clear day in good weather.

Plotting out your course and then keeping a dead-reckoning plot of your progress in good visibility lets you check your accuracy. Compass bearings are easy to get, and you can see how accurate they are. A few practice trips on the water and you will develop your skills to the point where you have confidence that the information you are writing on the chart corresponds to reality.

PRACTICE PLOTTING

The best way to practice is by doing, so let's see what is involved plotting a run from Solomons Island out into the Chesapeake Bay and then return. We're on a 28-foot cruising sailboat that can make 6 knots under power. We are assuming that there is a very light wind and so our trip will be made under power alone. If you have a faster boat, then the effects of current on your boat will be less, but the principles are the same.

Our point of departure is the flashing red light "6" guarding the shoal off the harbor entrance. From that point we want to go past Drum Point light "4" into the bay and then proceed northeast to can "77" off Little Cove Point. From there down the Bay to buoy "HI" off Hooper Island and back to Drum Point. All in all, it's a run of about 13 nautical miles that should take about two and a half hours. Departure is set for 0900, when the tide is high and the current slack.

Before leaving, let's plot the day's cruise on the chart. Assuming you are using the protractor parallel rule, place the straightedge of the plotter 1/4 inch or so south of light "6" and 1/4 inch south of Drum Point light "4," because we want to pass to seaward of both these lights. Then draw a straight line between these points.

Place the plotter over your mark close to "6" and align the grid on the plotter with the latitude or longitude lines on the chart. Make sure that the plotter's north is facing the top of the chart. Then read the true course from the edge of the plotter, which is at the intersection of the course line and the edge of the plotter. It should read 78 degrees. This is the true heading, but we have to correct it to the magnetic heading we use with the compass. Take a look over at the compass rose and note that there is a 10-degree west variation in this area. So add 10 degrees to the true course to get the compass course to steer. Assuming that your compass is accurate and you don't have to correct for deviation, write the 88-degree course above the line as "88M," meaning 88 degrees magnetic. If your compass had a deviation error, that should be applied to the magnetic heading to get the compass heading and plotted with a "C" for compass.

Now take the dividers and go to the distance scale on the chart and spread them to a convenient distance. In this case it's a mile. Put the point of the divider on the beginning of your course line at "6" and then move the other point in alignment with the course line. Note that the point of the divider is past Drum Point, so the distance must be less than a mile. Close the dividers slightly until the point of the divider is on Drum Point. Move the divider back to the scale and place one point on the zero and read the distance at the other point, which is about .95 nautical mile. Write this number under the course line as ".95NM."

You now have the first course and distance plotted on the chart. The other course from Drum Point to can "77" is 3.9NM on a course of 65 degrees magnetic. From there you turn south to a magnetic course of 155 degrees and stay on it for 3.25NM. Finally at "HI" turn eastward to a course of 285 magnetic for 5.2NM.

Now that everything is plotted, it is time to get going. Let's say that everyone is on time and ready to go at the first mark "6" at 0900. We put the boat on course 88 degrees and start out at 6 knots. It should take us just under ten minutes to come abeam of Drum Point. A look at the chart shows the water to be deep right up to the shore, and there are no other dangers that we should avoid along our track.

The run to Drum Point is short and the point is visible all the way, so there is no need to take a fix on other navigation aids to confirm progress, but we decide to practice using our hand bearing compass. A sighting on the square green daymark "1" visible north of our track is 322 degrees. Since this bearing is a compass or magnetic bearing, we have to convert it to a true bearing to plot it on the chart. If you look at the compass rose you see that 322 degrees on the inner magnetic rose is opposite the 312-degree mark on the outer compass ring. The true bearing from our boat to "1" is 312 degrees.

To plot this on the chart, place the center of the plotter on the "1," and check that it is properly orientated to the north and aligned with the latitude or longitude lines on the chart. Then make a mark at the edge of the plotter at the 313 degree mark. You will notice that this bearing is from the boat to the mark and what we want to plot is the bearing from the mark to the boat. This bearing is the reciprocal of 312 or 132 degrees.

The reciprocal of any course is 180 degrees from the bearing. To calculate the reciprocal, if the bearing is more than 180 degrees, subtract 180 from it; if less, add 180 to it.

To plot this bearing on the chart, make a mark opposite the 132-degree line on the edge of the plotter. Then use the edge of the plotter to draw a line from the center of the mark through the point. This line will cross the course plotted on the chart. The bear-

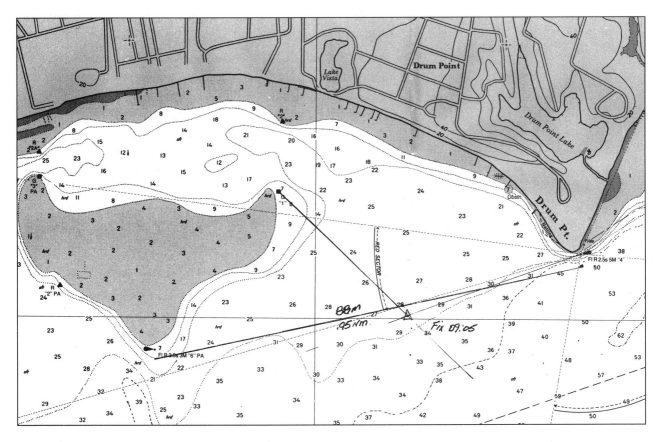

ing from daymark "1" will tell us how far along our course plot we have traveled, but will not help us determine if we are still on course.

If at the same time we took the bearing on "1" we also took a bearing on Drum Point light "4" and plotted it along with the "1" bearing, we could tell how far to the right or left of the course we are. The point where the bearing from "1" and "4" cross indicates our position at the time the bearings were taken, which is called a fix.

Let's say the hand bearing compass gave us a bearing of 81 degrees to Drum Point light. Remember to subtract 10 degrees to get the true bearing of 71 degrees true. The reciprocal of 71 is 251, which we plot on the chart. We now have a fix that puts us a little over halfway to Drum Point and a bit south of our intended track.

At about 0910 we come abeam of Drum Point light and swing north out into the Chesapeake Bay on a new course of 65 degrees magnetic. It is 3.9NM to can "77," so we settle back for the forty-minute run. After about twenty-five minutes we notice a tank on the shore close to Cove Point and find it on the chart. Bearings taken on the tank and the nun "2" will make a good fix. We take the bearing of "2" first because it is off the bow, so its bearing changes slowly as we move along our course. The hand bearing compass reads 58 degrees. We then take the bearing of the tank, which is changing faster, since it is coming abeam. It is 340 degrees.

When taking bearing on landmarks or aids to navigation, use the compass rose to convert the magnetic bearing read off the hand bearing compass to the true bearing needed to plot on the chart.

Plotting this fix, we change the magnetic bearings into true bearings by subtracting 10 degrees so the true bearing to "2" is 48 degrees, and we plot the reciprocal of 228 degrees. We plot the bearing to the tank by converting its magnetic bearing to a true bearing of 330 and then plot its reciprocal 164 on the chart.

This fix shows us more than halfway to "77" but a bit south and behind our intended track. We would have expected to travel about 2.5NM in the twenty-five minutes since we left Drum Point, but we have actually traveled 2.3NM. Probably the tide has started out and we are being set a bit to the south by it. By now we can see "77" and can steer directly for it. We notice that the new course is about 62 degrees on the compass, a bit west of our original course.

As we turn around "77" and pick up our new course of 155 to cruise down the bay, we notice that there is a wake behind "77," telling us that the tide has indeed begun to flow out of the bay. . Since we are running with the tide, we decide that it it not necessary to make any correction in our course down to "HI." But looking ahead, we see that on the run back to the Solomons we will have the current abeam for almost the whole leg, and it will have some effect.

A fix from plotting bearings from the tank and nun N "2" confirms that we are close to our intended course. Whenever possible, check your position by taking bearings on landmarks and aids to navigation.

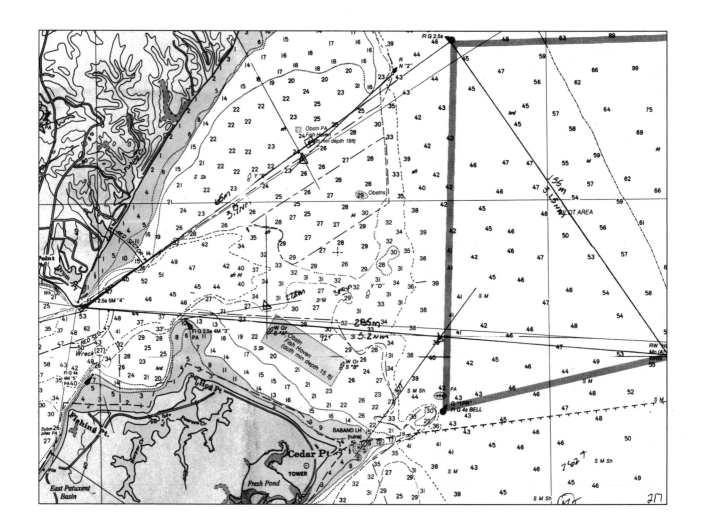

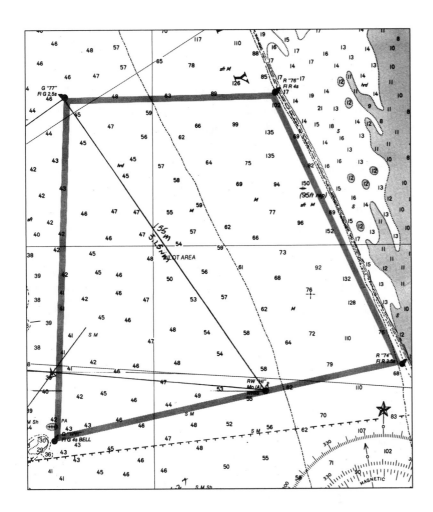

The course protractor will show the bearing from can G "77" to mid-channel marker "HI" is 165 degrees. This area has a 10-degree east variation, so you must subtract 10 degrees to find the compass course to steer. Write this above the course line as 155M.

While someone else steers the boat down the bay, let's look at the effect that the outgoing tide will have on our run back to Drum Point. First of all, we saw by the water flowing past "77" that the current is running in a southerly direction at about ¹/₂ knot. A look at the chart tells us that the current is most likely flowing on a heading of about 165 true or thereabouts. If we were to stop our engine and drift with the current, we would travel about ¹/₂ nautical mile along a course of 165 degrees. The distance we have to run back to Drum Point is 5.2NM, which will take us fifty minutes at our present speed. So during the time we are heading back to Drum Point, the water we are in is drifting along at ¹/₂ knot on a heading of 165.

If we steer our plotted course, then it stands to reason that we will end up south of Drum Point, possibly risking a grounding at Hog Point. To calculate how much we should correct our course to the north to compensate for the current, we make an easy-to-construct vector diagram. Of course, if you are a high school trigonometry whiz kid you can figure this out with a pocket calculator, but for us, a simple diagram is sufficient.

First, let's figure out how far we will drift. We will travel for fifty minutes back to Drum Point, and the tide moves at ¹/₂ knot an hour. Since time × speed = distance, we can calculate how far the tide will move during this time. Since speed is expressed in knots and these are nautical miles per hour, our formula must change hours into minutes. D in nautical miles = T in minutes × S in knots ÷ 60. So we solve the equation $D = 50 \times {}^{.5}/_{60}$ to get D = .4 nautical miles. This is the distance the water will move in fifty minutes.

Since it moves along a 165 course, we can plot where the boat will be in relation to Drum Point if you were to steer 285 degrees for fifty minutes while the water moves .4NM on a 165-degree course. To do this, place your plotter over Drum Point and lay out a line 165 degrees true from Drum Point. Then set your dividers to .4 nautical miles from the distance scale and place one point on Drum Point and the other on the line you just drew. Mark where the compass point rests on the line with a pencil. This is the point you will end up at if you don't correct for current set.

Draw a straight line from the point you just made on the tidal drift line back to the start of the leg from "HI." This line is the track the boat will actually follow through the water even though you are steering 285 degrees on your compass.

A current will set your boat off course. To figure out how to compensate for current set is not difficult using simple geometry to construct a vector diagram.

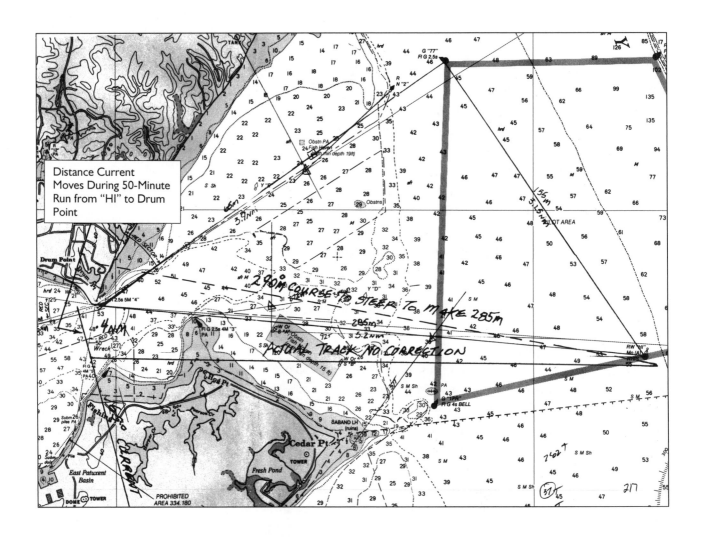

Distance Current Moves During 50-Minute Run from "HI" to Drum Point

It stands to reason that if you steer to the north of your course the exact amount that the current is setting you south, you will stay on course. As you can see, the real course made good is 270 true or 280 magnetic about 5 degrees south of your intended course. To correct for current set, steer a course 5 degrees north of your track, or 290 degrees.

We're getting close to "HI," and we want to get a good look at the current as we round the buoy and begin our new corrected course of 290. Sure enough, our estimates of the current strength must be pretty close, since it took us less than the 32 minutes we figured this leg would take at 6 knots. A look at the watch tells us that it took us less than 30 minutes for a speed close to 6 1/2 knots even though our knot meter read 6 all the way. If our instruments are correct, the only explanation for the difference is that the current is giving us a bit of a push. Of course, we would not be so lucky if we were going in the other direction.

After about 20 minutes on a course of 290 back to Drum Point, we decide to take a fix using the abandoned lighthouse off Cedar Point and the buoy "A" at the west edge of the fish trap area off Hog Point. The hand bearing compass shows the lighthouse bears 227 and buoy "A" 282. The fix puts us right on course.

At the beginning of this leg, a 5-degree compensation was applied to the course to offset current set. A fix off Cedar Point confirms our expected position, but the fix off Hog Point shows we have drifted north of the track. Always confirm your progress with fixes.

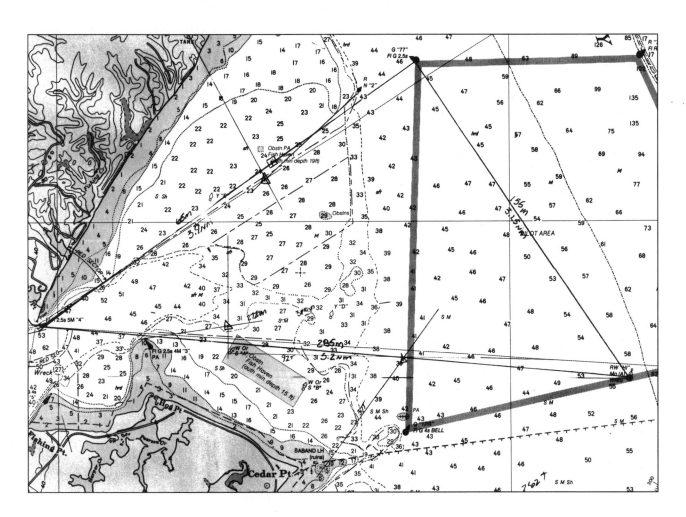

We continue on, and as we come abeam of "A," we seem to be passing too far to the north, so we take a quick bearing on "3," the light off Hog Point. Sure enough, it bears 272, and when plotted with the 180 bearing to "A" we find ourselves about 300 yards north of our track. The current must be less as we approach the mouth of the Patuxent River. In fact, we will probably be facing a current running out of the river by now. Of course, Drum Point is in sight, and we will not have any trouble finding our way back.

A run like this in good weather lets you practice piloting skills so when the fog rolls in and the visibility is poor, you're confident you know how to plot a course.

A depth sounder is also a great aid in navigating, because it provides information on the water depth to compare with the charted depths. For example, after passing Drum Point looking for "2" on the way to "77" in fog, we could look at the water depth. If it suddenly jumped from 25 feet to 18 feet we could tell we were on the ledge that's just north of "2."

Loran or GPS receivers calculate your boat's position continuously with relation to the ground, not the water, so by plotting the positions they produce on the chart and comparing them with your dead reckoning plot you can see the effect of current on your boat's progress. These electronics indicate your course made good over the bottom, which you can compare to your planned track. But no matter how sophisticated these electronic devices become, if you don't plot your position or at least write it down on a regular basis you're left staring at a blank chart when the electronics stop working.

ELECTRONIC NAVIGATION

VHF RADIOS

The VHF (very high frequency) radio is probably the most important piece of safety gear you can have on your boat. It uses very high frequencies that provide reliable communications over about 25 miles. VHF radios transmit and receive line-of-sight signals, so the curvature of the earth and mountains and hills stop VHF radio waves. VHF receivers are also designed to filter out all but the strongest signal. This allows several boaters to use the same frequency even if they are within the reception area of one another's radios. Consequently, VHF radios are used by thousands of boaters all over the world without interference problems. But even with the built-in advantages of this technology, marine radio frequencies are becoming more crowded. To operate a VHF radio you must have a licence issued by the Federal Communications Commission.

CONSOLE MOUNTS

Full-size VHF radios are getting smaller and less expensive every year. Today there is a VHF radio to fit even the smallest boat and budget. Any boat with a 12-volt battery and a place to erect the antenna can accommodate a console VHF radio.

VHF radios are a mature marine electronics category. Manufacturers have been improving radios for the last couple of decades, so even the least expensive units come standard with all the U.S. transmit and receive channels and receive-only weather channels built in.

Since the main purpose of the radio is safety, its reliability is of utmost importance. Unless the radio will be installed in the shelter of an enclosed bridge, its long-term reliability will be determined by how well it can stand up to moisture, an occasional drenching, and direct exposure to the sun.

Mount a console VHF radio where it is easy to access from the cockpit or the bridge. Try to install it out of the weather. Otherwise select a waterproof model.

A look at the manufacturer's warranty will give you a good idea of how well the unit is weatherized. Some radios are rated as splashproof and other are guaranteed waterproof for three years or longer. Most radio manufacturers now offer a flat-rate repair charge for out-of-warranty service.

The installation of your radio will to a great extent determine how well it will perform. When you press the transmit button on your radio it generates about 25 watts of radio frequency energy, but this energy will not be radiated very far unless the set is connected to an efficient antenna. Attention must be paid to installing the antenna system, which is made up of the antenna and mount and the coaxial cable connecting the radio to the antenna.

Marine antennas come in different lengths and are rated in decibels (db) according to their radiation pattern. A change of 3db represents a doubling of the antenna gain or its effective radiating efficiency. Very short 1-foot emergency antennas have no gain and are rated at 0db. These antennas radiate the radio energy generated by your radio equally in all directions. A good portion of this energy goes up into the sky and is wasted. By increasing antenna length, radio engineers are able to design antennas that don't radiate their energy evenly in all directions. These antennas radiate a stronger signal in the horizontal direction at right angles to the antenna, and thus more of the radio frequency energy is directed at the receiving station. This increase in effective power is called gain. As the length of the antenna increases, more and more energy is radiated in the horizontal plane and the antenna has a higher gain.

Standard 3-foot antennas have about twice the gain of the short emergency antennas, about 3db. Eight-foot and longer antennas have higher gains, in the 6-to-9db range. When comparing antennas, keep in mind that VHF is a line-of-sight transmission. On small boats, antenna height basically determines the effective range. Locating a 3db antenna on top of a sailboat's mast will increase the range more than mounting a higher-gain antenna on the stern pulpit a few feet off the water.

The motion of a smaller boat in a seaway will also effect the antenna's performance. Higher-gain antennas in the 6-to-10 db range have a narrow radiation pattern perpendicular to the antenna. This narrow pattern gives the antenna its gain but can cause reception problems when the boat rolls in heavy seas or when a sailboat heels over in a breeze.

The coaxial cable connecting the radio to the antenna is an often overlooked but important part of the antenna system. Many antennas are supplied with RG58 coaxial cable, which is adequate for short runs between the radio and antenna. For example, on a center-console boat with its radio and antenna installed on the console, the cable is okay, but for a longer run, consider using RG8 or its equivalent, in a high-performance, low-loss coaxial cable. Also, use as little solder on coaxial fittings as possible between the radio and the antenna. If the coaxial fittings are exposed to the weather, seal the fittings with heat-shrink tubing or wrap them tightly with waterproof tape to prevent internal corrosion.

HANDHELD UNITS

In addition to the full-size VHF radio, handheld VHF radios have become popular. These small radios have all the functions of the larger fixed-mount units with the exception of range. Handheld radios are limited to transmitters of 6 watts or less and generally have

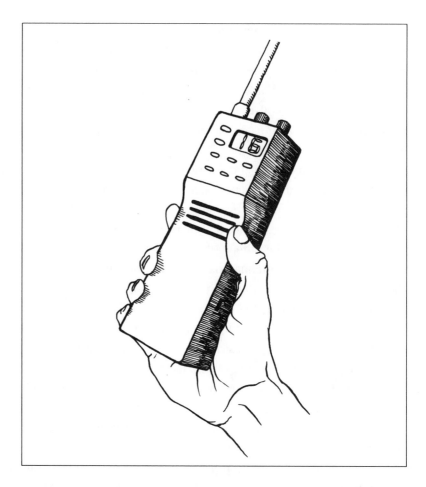

While its range is not as great as that of a console-mount VHF, the handheld VHF is ideal as an auxiliary unit and when used within close range.

a range of a couple of miles with the small no-gain antennas. Hand-helds can be connected to standard antennas to increase their range.

These portable radios run on rechargeable battery packs. Most come with recharging stands to hold the radio when it is recharging. Battery life can be lengthened if the low-power transmitter setting is used whenever possible.

TALKING ON A VHF RADIO

There's a certain etiquette to follow when communicating on a VHF radio. You initiate calls on Channel 16, and when contact is made you "switch and answer" on a working channel. Ask the Coast Guard or a marina in your area what are the working channels designated for boaters' communication and use them for your conversation after initiating the call on Channel 16. Use Channel 16 only to initiate a call. Don't use it for conversation, because it is designated for distress calls.

For example, if you're aboard *Gusto* and want to call the boat *Aquarius,* you use Channel 16, and the conversation goes something like this:

GUSTO:	*Aquarius, Aquarius*, this is *Gusto* WZP8380 calling, over.
AQUARIUS:	*Gusto*, this is *Aquarius* WXY2132, switch and answer on six-eight [meaning Channel 68].
GUSTO:	Roger, *Aquarius*, this is *Gusto* switching to six-eight.

Both boaters switch to Channel 68 and continue:

AQUARIUS:	*Gusto*, this is *Aquarius* on six-eight.
GUSTO:	*Aquarius*, this is *Gusto*.

Their conversation continues until completed. Then they say:

AQUARIUS:	*Gusto*, this is *Aquarius*, out, switching back to Channel 16.
GUSTO:	*Aquarius*, this is *Gusto*, roger that, switching back to Channel 16.

In your area, you'll find that certain channels are designated for bridge tenders and commercial vessel communications, so use them only for those purposes.

To make a distress call because of imminent danger that is life-threatening, use Channel 16 and repeat, "Mayday, Mayday, this is *Gusto* WZP8380 calling on sixteen." Wait for a response from the Coast Guard, and when it acknowledges, state the emergency, where your boat is located, the number of people aboard, and a description of the boat. You may receive help from the Coast Guard, its USCG Auxiliary, or a commercial towing craft that charges a fee for assistance.

SPEEDOMETER AND LOG

One of the most useful aids to navigation is an accurate speedometer and/or log. A speedometer registers how fast a boat is moving through the water, and a log records how far a boat has traveled. If either of these facts is known, the other can be calculated.

If you have carefully calibrated your tachometer by timing runs at different RPMs, then you can use your tachometer as a speedometer. However, marine growth on the bottom of the boat or the propeller can cause the boat to run slower than predicted. A calibrated speedometer measures the actual speed of the boat through the water, so it will read accurately no matter what the condition of the boat is.

Today most speedometers and logs are electronic. Most of them count the revolutions of a small paddle wheel. The faster the water moves past the boat's hull, the faster it turns this small wheel. Once each revolution, an electric pulse is sent to its central processing unit, where solid-state circuitry counts the pulses and calculates speed. At the same time it also sends a signal to the log unit, which uses the data to calculate the distance traveled through the water.

Since the small paddle wheel in the sending unit only reacts to water passing by the boat, it can measure speed and distance traveled through the water, but it can't provide information on speed or distance over the bottom. For example, if you were anchored in a 2-knot current the speedometer would indicate that the boat was going 2 knots through the water, because as far as the paddle wheel is concerned it is. However, a quick glance over at the shore will tell you that you are not moving over the bottom. The log will also record that your boat traveled 2 nautical miles at the end of an hour.

There are a few speedometers on the market that are self-powered and do not require an outside source of electricity, but most units need a source of 12-volt power. Speedometers don't draw much current themselves, usually much less than 1 amp, but those with built-in night lighting can. Most electric-starting outboards and engines equipped with an alternator would not have any problem keeping the battery charged.

Once calibrated, speedometers are usually trouble-free. You have to keep the sending unit free of marine growth, but the small paddle wheel usually stops rotating if it becomes fouled and the unit stops working. The sending unit can usually be removed from its through-hull housing for cleaning. It is a good idea to remove the sending unit from the through-hull fitting if the boat is not going to be used for a long time to prevent the buildup of marine growth on the unit.

A speed log with a through-hull fitting measures speed and distance traveled through the water.

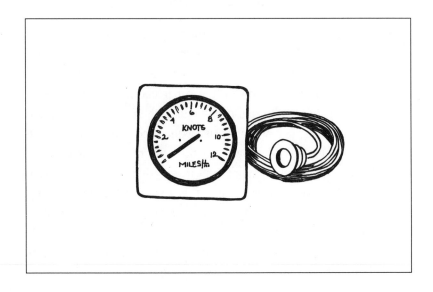

If you have a small boat with limited space for mounting electronic gear, consider multifunction instruments. Many manufacturers offer combined speed and log instruments; some also include a depth finder. Most units today have digital readout as opposed to an analog or dial-type display. Most digital units will handle speeds up to about 50 knots, so they can be used on both powerboats and sailboats. Analog units, however, are limited by the calibration of their display. Most units today are waterproof. Weathertightness is of utmost importance on a small boat, since the unit will eventually get wet.

DEPTH SOUNDER

The most reliable depth sounder found on any boat is a lead line. This simple device consists of a weight tied to the end of a piece of line. It has been used for centuries to measure water depth in coastal waters. A lot more convenient and just as accurate, a modern depth sounder uses sound to measure water depth.

There are a vast array of depth sounders on the market with analog, digital, and graphical displays. Even though these units may look different they all operate on the same principal: Sound travels through water at a constant speed.

A send/receive unit mounted underwater on the hull first sends out a high-frequency burst of sound. Then it waits for the sound to bounce off the bottom and return. The time it takes for the sound

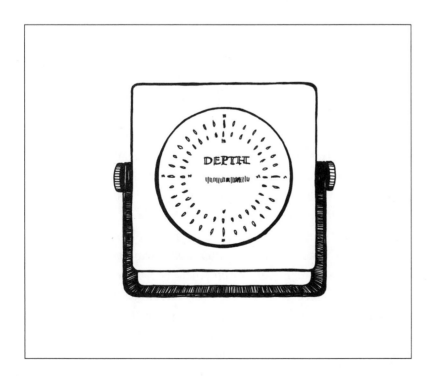

A flasher-type depth sounder uses a neon tube or LED that flashes next to the water depth. Small objects like fish will return dim flashes above the bottom. Newer models have multicolored displays.

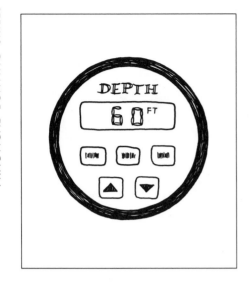

A digital depth sounder uses solid-state circuitry to convert the time delay directly into a number display that is easy to read even in direct sunlight.

to travel to the bottom and back is measured by the unit and converted into water depth.

The operation of the older flasher-type units is evident from a close look at the dial. A neon tube rotates at a steady rate behind the face of the unit. As the tube passes the top of the dial or zero depth, the sending unit flashes the tube and transmits a sound burst. The receiver flashes the tube as soon as the sound returns to the boat. During this time the neon tube is rotating. The deeper the water, the longer the sound takes to return and the farther the neon tube travels before it flashes. The dial is calibrated with markings to indicate the depth.

Since the neon tube flashes anytime a signal is returned to the unit, this type of display can indicate fish and other objects floating underwater. They appear as weaker flashes between the strong sending flash at the top of the dial and the bright bottom flash. Some units have different-colored neon tubes to indicate water depth and fish.

Digital-display depth sounders do not use a neon tube. Instead they use solid-state circuitry to convert the time delay directly into a number display. This type of unit is easiest to read in direct sunlight but does not provide much information on whether there are fish or other submerged objects in the water under your boat.

All depth sounder use an underwater transducer to send and receive the sound signals. These can be mounted through the hull or on the transom. To lessen drag in the water, the transducer can also be mounted inside a solid fiberglass hull. In this type of installation the transducer is placed inside a liquid-filled vault that is bonded to the hull, which reduces drag, along with the performance of the depth finder.

FISHFINDER

The fishfinder is nothing more than a very sophisticated depth sounder. The circuitry is tuned to be more sensitive to weak returning signals that bounce off fish. Many of the first commercial units recorded the depth and fish information graphically on paper. The paper strip formed a picture of the bottom as the boat moved over it. Today most fishfinders designed for small boats have either a liquid crystal display (LCD) like a portable computer or video game, or a cathode ray tube (CRT) display like a television. The LCD displays use less electricity, can be made completely waterproof, and are compact and probably better suited for small boats.

Both the depth sounder and the fishfinder can be used as valuable aids to navigation by looking at the water contour and depths noted on a chart and comparing them with the readout on the instrument.

For example, let's say the entrance to your harbor has a breakwater that extends out from the shore in an east-west direction to about 30 feet of water. You note that the 30-foot depth is rather constant for several miles to the north and south of the entrance. If the fog rolls in and you know your position is south of the breakwater, you can head east toward the shore until you reach 30 feet of water. Then turn north and continue adjusting your course slightly to stay in 30 feet of water. Keep a sharp lookout, because you will eventually run right into the end of the breakwater. Of course, if you're in tidal waters, consider the rise and fall of the tides.

Both the depth sounder and the fishfinder will give you this valuable navigational information. Even if you're not a serious angler, some of the newer fishfinders have a graphical display that not only shows water depth and fish but also shows course, speed, and location information from a Loran or GPS receiver. This single graphical display may replace several hard-to-read displays that are cluttering up your helm station.

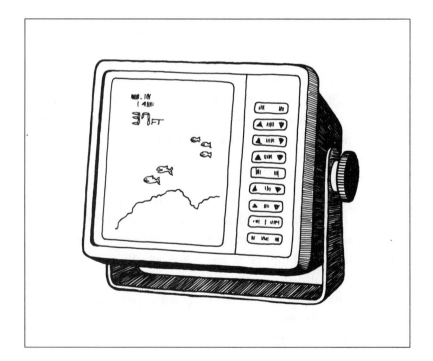

A fishfinder uses the same circuitry as a depth sounder, tuned to be more sensitive. It can have either an LCD or a CRT display.

LORAN-C AND GPS

Unlike a speedometer or log, both Loran-C and GPS (Global Positioning System) receivers tell you how your boat is moving relative to the earth. Direction, speed, and position are calculated relative to a known location on the earth, so this information represents movement over the bottom, not through the water.

These receivers calculate the distance and bearing to a location entered called a way point. This is especially useful for sailboaters who make numerous tacks when sailing to a destination upwind. Latitude and longitude positions are also in reference to movement over the bottom, and the course and speed actually made good over the bottom are calculated by the GPS or Loran-C receiver. Comparing this information to your dead reckoning plot allows you to calculate the set and drift of the current.

Loran-C and GPS make navigating much easier and safer. These receivers are very reliable, but like anything electronic on a boat, they can and will eventually stop working. There are warnings printed on every navigational chart cautioning the navigator not to rely on a single aid to navigation. The same holds true for relying exclusively on electronic navigation. If you're prudent, maintain a current track on the chart and update it at least once an hour. And check your position occasionally by taking bearings off navigational aids or landmarks to compare with your charted position. Should the Loran-C or GPS decide to stop, you can continue navigating by dead reckoning and your position on the chart will not be more than an hour old. If you don't want to take the time to plot your track on the chart, at least enter your position in the log so you can go back and plot the information if the need arises.

LORAN-C

Loran is an electronic navigation system that uses low-frequency radio waves to compute a fix. The system was developed by the U.S. government during the Second World War. The original Loran-A system has been replaced throughout the world, except in Japan, by Loran-C.

A Loran master station transmits a pulsed radio signal, which is followed by transmissions from several other slave stations that make up a Loran chain. The Loran receiver calculates the time difference between the arrival of the master and slave signals and computes its fix which is accurate to about 1/10 nautical mile in good conditions. Inaccuracies are caused by the radio waves traveling over landmasses. However, the conditions that cause these inaccuracies are constant, so the Loran receiver can return to within 50 feet of a previously recorded fix. This makes Loran the system to use to return to a favorite fishing hole.

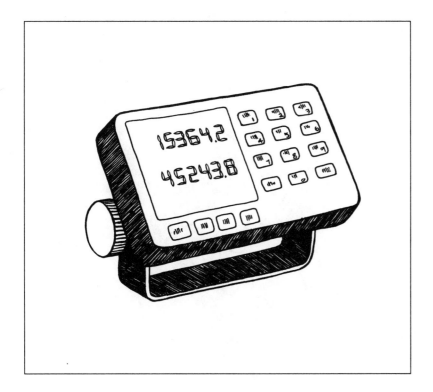

A Loran receiver computes a fix to within 1/10 nautical mile in good conditions, making it a powerful instrument for returning to a favorite anchorage or fishing hole.

The price of Loran receivers has fallen in the last decade, and today a full-featured Loran-C receiver can be purchased for less than $225. Part of the reason for the drop in Loran-C prices is that GPS has become operational and will eventually replace Loran-C.

The price of GPS receivers has fallen to the point where it is comparable to that of high-end Loran sets. But for the skipper who operates a small boat in an area with good Loran coverage and will probably never need worldwide coverage, a Loran set is still probably the best choice. Loran-C sets are better at returning to a pre-recorded location, so if you navigate to familiar locations a Loran set will give you better results. The sets are available in very small watertight units that are ideal for mounting on a small boat.

Loran-C sets are subject to interference from other radio transmissions, so before purchasing a set, check with someone who is using Loran in your area to find out if there are any reception problems. Most Loran-C sets come with a set of pretuned filters, but some areas of the country require special filters for best reception. They also require an antenna. There are multipurpose VHF/Loran antennas available that can simplify the installation of a radio and Loran on a small boat.

GPS

The Global Positioning System was developed and is maintained by the U.S. Department of Defense. GPS receivers give you the same navigational information as a Loran-C set, except the system has

A handheld GPS (Global Positioning System) receiver acquires high-frequency radio signals from orbiting satellites. Many of these portable devices operate on rechargeable batteries and have a built-in antenna.

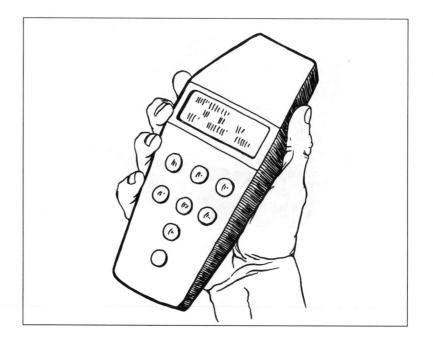

worldwide coverage. Orbiting satellites transmit high-frequency radio signals to the GPS receiver, allowing it to calculate a fix. The receiver must be able to acquire the signal of at least three satellites to obtain an accurate fix. Generally, a GPS set can deliver a fix that is within 300 feet of its true location anywhere on the globe. In many cases the receiver will be even more accurate.

Besides providing worldwide coverage, GPS navigation systems are generally more accurate navigating to plotted locations than Loran-C receivers, which makes GPS a better choice for the boater cruising to destinations far from home port and operating in unfamiliar waters where there are no prerecorded fixes to navigate to.

GPS receivers come in all shapes and forms, including handheld units that make installation on a small boat very easy. Most of the handhelds can operate on rechargeable batteries or on internal power from a boat's 12-volt system. The handheld units have a built-in antenna. If a portable unit is mounted below deck in the cabin, it requires an external antenna. GPS antennas are only 4 to 6 inches in diameter and 4 to 12 inches high, which is a lot smaller than a Loran-C or VHF antenna. The antenna should be mounted so that it has a clear view of the horizon in all directions.

CRUISING

An inflatable dinghy is a popular accessory for transportation ashore and discovering shallow waters when at anchor.

Gone cruising means many things to many boaters. For some it's the great escape from work and commitments, and for others it's a short getaway to enjoy being on the water. Both powerboat and sailboat enthusiasts enjoy being on the water and the daily challenge of choosing a destination and then reaching it. Whether it's for faraway places or close to home harbors, cruising plans should start with preparation and should involve everyone aboard.

SYSTEMS CHECK

Check that the boat and equipment are in good working order so you won't have to deal with breakdowns or equipment failure. Inspect the motor to see that its parts and pumps are working. Check the oil, water, and transmission fluid levels. Check to see that batteries are fully charged, and check the water level in the battery.

Check your supply of spare parts (filters, gaskets, and hose clamps). Look at pumps and hoses to see that they are clear and run free, and reroute any that are kinked. Check that they are connected securely.

If you have a sailboat, make sure that the sails are not frayed or torn and that the rigging works freely. See that you have spare battens and fittings and an extra jib line.

Make sure that the running lights are operating, and if you have an older boat with fuses rather than circuit breakers, check the fuses and have a supply of spare ones on board.

Double-check that the head works properly. Keep a spare parts kit that includes gaskets and impellers along with treatments or chemicals for the head.

In the galley, check the supply of cooking fuel (LPG, alcohol, or kerosene) to make sure that there's a full tank. If your stove lights with a match, bring some matches in an airtight container or a butane lighter.

If you have a refrigeration system, make sure that it's working properly and draining. Have a spare parts kit that includes impellers. If you have an icebox, lay in a good supply of ice in both blocks and cubes.

Inspect all safety gear and make sure that the communication equipment, especially the VHF radio, is operational. If you have a handheld VHF, bring fresh or newly recharged batteries to operate it.

The anchor should always be ready to drop in case of an emergency, so make sure that it is stowed in a convenient locker, not buried and difficult to reach. Keep the anchor line handy and untangled, too.

If you leave your dock lines attached to the slip, bring along dock lines and fenders for tying up in a marina slip.

If the topsides are dirty, give the boat a good cleaning and hose it down. Some boaters like to clean their boat after duffel bags and food sacks have been loaded on board, because all the foot traffic brings aboard land dirt.

Just before leaving, top off the water tanks and take garbage ashore. Then stop at the gas dock and top off the fuel tank and empty the head's holding tank.

SHIP'S PAPERS

Get papers in order and consolidated in a notebook designated "Ship's Papers." Use a pocket notebook or a binder with clear plastic envelope sheets to organize material about the operating systems of the boat. These include manuals, boat and VHF radio registration papers, the name of your insurance agent, and any other important papers associated with the boat.

▲ ▲ ▲

FOUL-WEATHER GEAR

A suit of foul-weather gear including jacket, bib pants, and sea boots is an investment you'll make once that will pay back for years to come. The fabrics include PVC (polyvinyl chloride), polyurethane (a rubber polymer) and neoprene. PVC is lightweight, has welded seams, and comes in a variety of qualities. Polyurethane is more flexible and breathable than PVC. Neoprene, the most expensive, is the most flexible and durable and also the heaviest, so it's ideal for cold-weather boating.

If your boating is in warm weather, choose lightweight gear made of fabric that breathes so it doesn't get too hot to wear. No-nonsense PVC or the traditional yellow rubber suit is the least expensive. Those with cotton backing are cooler on the skin. These suits are ideal for fishermen, because they rinse clean easily.

A well-designed jacket is made of waterproof fabric with lined pockets, cuffs that can be sealed at the wrists, double flaps of Velcro closures over an oversized two-way zipper, and a fold-away hood with a visor. If you go boating at night, consider a jacket with reflective patches so it's visible in the dark.

Bib versus waist-high pants is a matter of preference. Bib pants with wide elasticized suspenders are probably the most popular, because they give you added protection from water creeping up your back and they let you bend and move without restrictions, so they're comfortable to wear. A well-designed pair of pants is made of waterproof fabric with cuffs that can be sealed or cinched over boots, pockets, and abrasive patches so you can kneel or sit on a slippery deck.

If the weather is cool in your area, consider a lined suit that keeps you dry with room for layers of clothing underneath.

For budget gear, pick up a PVC rain poncho with a hood that can be used as an instant solution to a sudden downpour, but it won't keep you protected and warm as a jacket and pants will.

Rubberized sea boots with sure-grip soles and mid-shin sides keep your feet dry and warm and provide traction on slippery decks.

▼ ▼ ▼

EAT HEARTY

When it comes to planning meals and filling the food lockers, boaters take a variety of approaches, which are largely dependent on how much they like to cook. (They all like to eat!) Some choose to eat out so they don't have to deal with cooking and washing dishes. They stock up with cereals, nibbling food, and beverages and plan to visit marinas and yacht clubs where they can eat out. Others use convenience foods that require little preparation and cleanup time. With a microwave oven and power to operate it, this approach works well. So does using the frozen boil-in-a-bag prepared entrees that require only a pan of boiling water.

Budget- and nutrition-conscious boaters often prepare meals in advance and freeze them. A frozen block of chili or spaghetti sauce can be heated for the night's fare and helps to keep other things cold, too. Make-ahead meals like meat loaf and pasta salad are easy to prepare at home and bring along.

Nothing beats the intoxicating smell of a barbecue grill, and many marinas have them available, complete with picnic tables. Just bring your own charcoal briquettes and lighter fluid.

If you do a lot of overnight anchoring, consider buying a marine barbecue grill designed for a boat. The unit is designed to mount on the railing with a sturdy bracket and has a kettle lid over a base unit that holds charcoal or an LPG cylinder for fuel. The grill is permanently installed and out of the way, yet convenient to use at mealtime. Many boaters prepare an entire meal on these handy grills, because cooking topsides keeps heat and congestion out of the galley. It also keeps unwanted food odors out of the cabin, which is difficult to air out and ventilate.

When you're looking for a place to eat ashore, ask a local boater at a marina where you're staying. You're likely to get a quick rundown of what's available within walking distance. Marina operators are another good source. And sometimes you'll see posters advertising a restaurant with a courtesy van that has a free pickup service for boaters.

GALLEY-WISE

To make sure that you haven't forgotten any food items when you're planning a cruise, start a list and add to it as you remember things you want to include. Lay out the "boat food" on a table to double-check you have everything you need before packing it for the boat.

▲ ▲ ▲

WATER BOTTLES

Individual water bottles are an alternative to cans of soda pop. The water is good for you, and it's a lot cheaper than soft drinks. Buy juice or water in individual-serving-size plastic bottles, and when they're empty, wash them out, fill them with water, and freeze them with the lids off. Leave about an inch of air space at the top of the bottle so the water can expand when it freezes. Bring the frozen bottles aboard and they'll thaw slowly while helping to keep your icebox cold. Refill them and you always have chilled water.

▼ ▼ ▼

Put the packages in piles according to how they will be served so you'll be reminded of condiments or special serving utensils you might need. Don't forget garbage bags and the can opener!

Canvas sacks are sturdy and convenient to carry food and beverage cans aboard, and they're handy to take ashore for shopping and laundry. Don't forget about dishwashing chores, which are not always easy in the confines of a small galley sink. One method is to fill a plastic dishpan with soapy water to wash the dishes, then rinse them in the sink and drain them on the counter.

If you have a limited water supply or "cold water only," consider serving frozen boil-in-a-bag entrees and save the hot water for dishwashing.

You don't have to load up a boat with a week's worth of food. It's fun to add variety to meals with local fresh produce such as melons, tomatoes, and corn that you can buy along the way. And remember, you don't have to chill all produce either. Use string bags hung from a handrail down below to hold bulky fruits and vegetables that haven't been refrigerated.

Whatever and however you eat, just plan on being hungry and thirsty much of the time, because being on the water stimulates the appetite.

Bring all the food destined for the refrigerator or icebox chilled, especially beverage cans. If you stock up with chilled food items, the system only has to maintain the degree of coldness and not work overtime. Bring aboard frozen plastic containers of water and beverages and any prepared entrees so they'll keep the box cooled while they defrost.

For a week aboard, it's a good idea to bring along a sidekick cooler for beverages that will be opened and closed several times a day. Stow it where it's easily accessible and out of the sun. Or use an extra cooler to store bulky frozen foods for dinner that you tuck out of the way because you'll open it less frequently. To maintain the cooler, drain off the water every few days (or as needed) and replenish with ice. The timing depends on the temperature of the water and the weather.

CREATURE COMFORTS

Follow the Scout motto, "Be prepared," and bring along things to do while you're under way—books, tapes, a cross-stitch project, plenty of activities for kids aboard. To keep from cluttering up the boat, assign a canvas sack to each crew member to stow the fun stuff.

Don't forget a pair of binoculars so you can spot navigational marks and signs along the way and follow the flight of birds and wildlife.

Some boats have enough storage space so bed linens or sleeping bags can be stowed when they're not being used, but on small boats, space is at a premium. To keep tight quarters neat and tidy, tuck folded sheets inside the case with the pillow and stow a folded blanket inside a pillowcase or sham; it can double as a pillow.

Bring clothes aboard in a duffel bag, and keep them there unless you have locker and drawer space. A laundry bag where everyone can stash dirty clothes and towels is handy, too. Don't forget a supply of old-fashioned wood clothespins for drying towels and swimsuits on the lifelines.

Most marinas have a shower room. Use a canvas sack to carry all the stuff you need: soap, shampoo, hair dryer, towel, and change of clothes.

LAUNDRY CHORES

If you bring enough clothes or live in a swimsuit, then you can probably avoid doing laundry. Many marinas feature coin-operated clothes washers and dryers, which is very convenient. Bring along a roll of quarters so you don't have to scrounge around for change. Take laundry soap premeasured for one load in a plastic sandwich bag so you'll have everything you need. Or load your dirty clothes into a pillowcase and pour the soap loose into the case. Toss it into the washing machine and it's ready to go.

NECESSARY AND NICE TO HAVE ABOARD

You can make a boat as comfortable and convenient as home while you're cruising by outfitting it with things you'll frequently use. Here's a list of items you'll find useful and helpful to have on board.

boat hook

fenders

compass

bailer

air horn

extra pump

paddle

BASIC FIRST-AID KIT

You can buy a marine first-aid kit or assemble one yourself using a plastic container with a tight-fitting lid that's easy to stow in a watertight compartment or locker. Customize the kit to suit the needs of your crew members with any medicine or prescriptions necessary. Here are some basics for a boat's medical kit:

motion-sickness tablets or bands

sunscreen

bug- and jellyfish-sting relief pads

aspirin

scissors

magnifying glass

tweezers

bandages of various sizes

gauze pads of various sizes and adhesive tape

zinc oxide

instant cold pack

wound wipes

burn ointment

first-aid cream or ointment

petroleum jelly

first-aid booklet or instructions

▼ ▼ ▼

swim ladder

bucket and mop

nylon fish-landing net

water hose with sprayer attachment

rechargeable flashlight

portable radio

portable CD player or tape deck

battery-driven flexible goose-neck clamp-on light

binoculars

net gear hammocks

portable tool tote

shock cords with hooks or hold-downs

12-volt or battery-driven cabin fan

compact 12-volt or motor-driven boat vacuum with crevice tool

nonskid welcome mat

first-aid kit and manual

playing cards and games

OUTDOOR LIVING

If you have a boat with an open cockpit where everyone seems to congregate, consider using a sunshade. It can be as simple as a golf umbrella lashed to a railing or as elaborate as a custom-made bimini or awning designed to shield your cockpit from sunlight and rain showers. And don't forget the sunscreen!

For the nighttime invasion of mosquitoes, gnats, and no-see-ums, consider adding screens to the hatchway and portholes. You can order these as accessories to fit a boat from most manufacturers or make them using screen kits. These kits include screening fabric that you cut to size and secure with a Velcro-like hook and tape.

Use bug repellent to rid the cockpit of pesky critters, or try using a laundry fabric-softener sheet like Downy. Rub the sheet on ankles, legs, and arms; the scent acts as a repellent. Save the sheets for reuse.

When there doesn't seem to be a breath of wind down below, add a wind scoop, which is a nylon cylinder for hatches designed to catch and funnel air.

KEEP A SOCIAL LOG AND TAKE PICTURES

It doesn't have to be fancy or long-winded, but a written log of the harbors and anchorages visited and new boating friends you met is a nice way to remember your cruise long after it's over. The log is also a handy reference to jot down notes about a harbor you might want to revisit. It can be as simple as a notebook where you jot down things to remember for your next cruise or the address of a new marine supplier you learned about talking to other boaters.

Bring along a camera to document your cruise and you'll enjoy reliving the cruise for years to come. If you're a know-nothing photographer, pick up a one-use-only camera; they're inexpensive and easy to use. If you're a photo buff, you'll enjoy creating interesting scenic shots and taking candid people pictures along the way. And if you have a videocamera you can make your own boating movies. No matter what level you're at, bring along some kind of camera and use it to capture your cruise.

TRAVELING WITH A BUDDY BOAT

Cruising with another boat is often fun, especially for first-time boaters who are hesitant to go out on their own. With a buddy boat you'll have a friend to rely on and someone to communicate with along the way. Rotate the positions of lead boat and keep in contact by monitoring a working frequency on the VHF while you're under way.

BE YOUR OWN CRUISE DIRECTOR

Chapter 12, on navigation, takes you through the basics of reading a nautical chart and plotting a course so you know the distance you'll travel and at what speed. Spend time at home planning with a nautical chart of your cruising area. Do your plotting and calculating when you have plenty of time to enjoy the exercise and familiarize yourself with the process. Mark the chart so it's ready for reference when you get under way.

Choose a destination that has a good safe harbor as well as shoreside activities, especially if you're cruising with children. Many marinas have swimming pools and rental bicycles available and are conveniently located near towns with restaurants and sites of interest.

If you'd like to know about shoreside activities in a particular area, call the area's visitors' bureau or chamber of commerce for information before you leave. Such offices usually send brochures and information about any regional fairs or festivals. You might want to join in with the crowd or avoid the congestion, so it helps to know in advance what's happening. Find the telephone number by calling the town or county office.

Choose a town that offers things your crew like to do. If there are tennis players aboard, plan to stop in a town marina with tennis courts nearby. If the skipper's idea of fun is puttering on the boat, make sure to bring along all the tools needed. If "shop till you drop" is the philosophy of some crew members, choose a destination with that in mind.

If space permits and you like to explore new areas, consider investing in a folding bicycle. These compact bikes are designed to be small and lightweight; some are "marinized" to withstand the corrosive marine environment. The bike can be equipped with a basket for carrying groceries and supplies, and can be stowed away in a locker or lashed down when the boat is under way.

OVERNIGHTING AT MARINAS AND CLUBS

The transient or visiting slip fee at many marinas and clubs is based on the length of the boat. Some charge additionally for electrical hookup. For example, at a marina charging $1 a foot and $3.50 electric, the one-night charge for a 30-foot boat is $33.50. Sometimes you have to pay a refundable deposit on the electrical cord needed to connect your power system to the marina's.

Before arriving at the dock of a marina or club, call the dockmaster on the VHF requesting permission for a slip and wait for directions about entering. Usually the dockmaster will assign you a slip and tell you where it's located. If you'd like someone to be there to catch your lines, ask for assistance.

If the dockmaster doesn't monitor the VHF, pull up to the gas dock and wait for an attendant.

During popular holiday weekends there's usually a minimum requirement of a two-day slip rental, and it's a good idea to book a reservation early.

If your boat doesn't have comfortable sleeping accommodations, make an advance reservation at a motel or inn that's within walking distance of a marina. Most marina operators can suggest nearby lodging if you call to reserve a slip.

CONSIDER BOAT CAMPING

In many cruising areas, there's a public park with a sandy beach where boaters can pitch a small tent to spend the night. Small boats may offer few or no accommodations, but boat camping is an affordable way to stay overnight without staying aboard. It's ideal for cruising with kids, who need to get off the boat and have room to roam. You need a tent and camping gear, and the space inboard to carry it, so the simpler the setup, the better.

Run the boat up on the beach and carry ashore an anchor. If the waters are tidal, put out a stern anchor as well.

Because of their shallow draft, houseboats are ideal for beaching along a sandy shoreline.

ON THE HOOK

If you prefer the peace and quiet of being at anchor, choose a protected cove with good holding ground. Before you leave port, look over a navigational chart of the cove to determine the best place to drop the hook. Consider the weather. If it's hot and muggy, don't anchor too close to shore, where breezes won't cool you; it's better to be out in more open waters. Choose an anchorage for its proximity to land if you want to go ashore or for the privacy and remoteness you might prefer. But first and foremost, always choose an anchorage for its protection from the wind and for its water depth.

As you prepare to leave an anchorage and "up anchor," don't forget you might be bringing more up on deck than just the anchor. If you have dropped the hook in a muddy bottom, some of that mud will be stuck to the anchor as it comes on deck. Have a bucket ready to splash down the anchor and decks to wash away the mud.

Plan the passage so you arrive early in the afternoon when the anchorage won't have filled up with boaters and you'll have more choice about where to drop the hook.

The logistics of stowing an anchor so it's always ready to drop depend on the size of your boat and the configuration and space at the bow pulpit. If there is plenty of space to stow the anchor on deck, use chocks mounted on deck. These chocks are made of either plastic resin or chrome-plated bronze and are screwed into the deck permanently. They are designed to hold Danforth-type anchors so they can be removed easily before anchoring. Another choice is a bow rail latch designed to hold Danforth and fluke-type anchors. The anchor hangs from a chock bracket mounted to the railing. This rig is ideal for small boats with little bow space because it gets the anchor off the deck.

If you don't plan to anchor very often, you can make your own chocks using the stanchions on the bow as posts by securing the anchor between them. Lash the shackle end of the shank to one stanchion and the stock end of the anchor to the other one, making sure that your knots are secured.

DO IT WITH A DINGHY

If you like to anchor out, having a dinghy gives you the freedom to go ashore wherever you've dropped the hook. Whether it's in a busy harbor town or at a quiet anchorage, a dinghy becomes your tender and lets you make trips ashore and explore the area. You can spend an afternoon trolling for a seafood dinner or venturing into a remote cove and up an uncharted creek.

There are choices to consider when it comes to dinghies. First, do you want a hard one made of fiberglass or wood or a soft inflatable boat? Then there's the issue of how to take it along. You can tow a dinghy behind a boat or stow it in davits on the stern or in chocks on the cabin house. And what about an outboard? It increases your range of dinghy travel, but storing and manhandling one is an issue.

First, let's consider the two types of dinghies. A hard-surface dinghy is stable and rigid, and many are designed as sailing dinghies and come equipped with a mast and sails. A fiberglass dinghy requires no maintenance and is lighter than a wooden one.

A rubber boat doesn't sail well and can be difficult to row, because it has no keel under the water to give it steerage. But its good points make it desirable as a dinghy for cruising. It's ideal for swimming off the boat, because it's like a big rubber raft—you can roll over the sides into the water and get back aboard just as easily. Those outfitted with floorboards are as stable as a hard dinghy. It can be stowed deflated or partially deflated so as to take up little space lashed on the deck. Or it can be kept in davits or towed.

The trick to towing any dinghy is to keep it riding on the back of the second wave of your wake. You have to experiment with the speed of your boat and sea conditions to get it right. You want to avoid having the dinghy too far behind caught in the trough of a wake, which sometimes lets the bow of the dinghy dive down and fill with water. But you don't want the dinghy to ride so close to the stern of your boat that it bangs into it when you slow down.

When stowed in davits on the stern, a dinghy is out of the way, yet readily available to use. You can launch and retrieve it using a simple block-and-tackle system. If you have a transom and swim platform, another type of davit system raises a dinghy up out of the water and stows it against the transom, resting on the swim platform.

If you want to carry a dinghy on the cabin house of a boat, you'll find specialty chock fittings for both inflatable and hard dinghies. This system works well with a sailboat with a mast and winch that lifts the dinghy out of the water with lines attached to it.

You can manpower a dinghy with rowing oars or use a small lightweight 2- or 3-horsepower outboard motor. To get the motor on and off the mother boat, you can muscle it down into the dinghy or use a hoist with a boom-and-tackle system. It mounts on the rails and swings out into the water with the outboard enclosed in a canvas sling. One person directs it from the boat, while another is in the dinghy ready to receive it.

If you use an outboard with a dinghy, check with local marine authorities to see if a license for the dinghy is required. In most states it is.

SECURITY WHILE CRUISING

"The best defense is a good offense" applies to securing a boat as well as to sports. If you make a boat difficult to break into by installing locks, you discourage intruders. You'll find keyed flush-mount locks and the traditional pad locks that operate with a key or number combination. Keyed-alike locks are handy on boats, be-

▲ ▲ ▲

RAFTING UP

If you want to raft up to an anchored boat for a few hours, approach it from downwind. Hang as many fenders as possible vertically on your boat and rig a bow, stern, and forward and after spring lines. Make an initial pass by the boat to talk to the skipper and be sure he is ready for you to come alongside.

Approach the anchored boat slowly and first pass your bow line and then your after spring line to the boat's crew member. After these are secured, position your boat so the spreaders are *not* aligned if the boats are sailboats or the boarding gates *are* aligned if they are powerboats. Then secure the forward spring and stern lines.

▼ ▼ ▼

cause one key opens all locks. Choose a lock that is brass or weather-resistant to withstand the harsh marine environment and add one to the companionway, on deck boxes, and on lazarette storage compartments. When you leave a boat, close and lock it.

To secure a movable object like a bicycle or outboard, use a vinyl-coated cable. Wind it through the object and a stanchion and secure its ends with a padlock. There are specialty keyed outboard motor locks that you install over the motor's mounting screws so it cannot be removed.

BRINGING ALONG PETS

Pets enjoy the boating life, too, so bring them along once they have their sea legs.

Dogs and cats are part of many boaters' families, so it's natural to bring them along. Some pets are born to be on the water, but others prefer land life. To find out how your pet fares, bring it along for the day before taking it on a week's cruise. If your pet has sea legs and enjoys being on a boat, include it in your cruise plans. Otherwise you're putting it in an uncomfortable position. It will be much happier with a pet sitter or in a kennel.

While you're under way, keep pets safe by watching their movements if they're free to roam or put them below where there's plenty of ventilation and water for drinking. If you let them roam the boat, keep them protected from the sun under a bimini top or sunshade. And when you pull into a dock, keep pets below or leashed so they can't jump ashore. Don't forget their favorite food and toys!

If you bring pets to a marina or yacht club, call first to see if they're welcome and if there are any conditions about being on a leash. Dogs need to go ashore, so it's good to know beforehand what the rules are.

Keep the cat's litter box in a safe protected area that's easy to clean.

KIDS ABOARD

If you're boating with infants, you'll need room to bring along all their stuff. Designate a "baby on board" area with good ventilation where they can safely take naps and where you can stow all of their stuff and change diapers. Outfit them in a personal flotation device that's designed to roll them over in the water, keeping the head supported and face up in the water. Kids of all ages should wear a safety vest that is comfortable and lightweight and use a safety harness to attach them to the boat. As an added safety measure, install netting around the boat in the gap between the lifelines and the deck. Netting comes 24 inches high in various lengths that can be run from bow to stern. It's especially effective on the bow, in the cockpit, on the flying bridge, or wherever there is any gap or opening. It's also helpful if you have pets.

TIPS FOR PLANNING A WEEKEND CRUISE

For a weekend aboard, don't venture too far from your home port—make it an easy passage. Choose a destination within a reasonable distance so you'll have time to enjoy your stay. The best way to learn about interesting weekend-away places is to talk to other boaters in your marina or yacht club and to read a regional boating magazine or cruising guide for the area you're in. You'll find a wealth of information about the harbors and anchorage as well as about the history of the area. Good cruising material gives the location of marinas as you approach the harbor and details their facilities. It describes the location of a designated anchorage with its water

HANGING ON TO YOUR HAT

To keep your hat from blowing off in a wind, attach it to a shirt collar with a hat clip, a short elastic cord with a tiny alligator-type clip at each end. Attach one end to your hat and the other to your shirt collar.

Or make your own hat clip with a short piece of string and a safety pin. Cut a string about 12 inches long and tie one end of the string to your hat and the other end to a safety pin. Put your hat on and then fasten the pin to the collar of your shirt. If you don't want to use a pin, then tie the string to a buttonhole in your shirt.

▲ ▲ ▲

FLAG ETIQUETTE

A burgee is a flag identifying a private club or organization and displayed on boats owned by members of the club.

The national ensign, which has thirteen red and white stripes and fifty white stars on a blue background, denotes the nationality of the boat's owner and was created to identify the origin of the boat.

A yacht ensign has a fouled anchor and thirteen stars in place of the fifty stars. It may be used in place of the national ensign when in domestic waters.

All ensigns should be flown until sunset.

On a powerboat, carry a club burgee on the bow and the ensign on the stern.

On a sloop-rigged sailboat, carry the club burgee at the masthead and the ensign on the stern or on the trailing edge of the sail.

▼ ▼ ▼

depth and tips about the bottom being good holding in clay or not so good and sandy. It includes information about shopping, museums, and places of interest you might want to visit.

When you are staying at a marina or yacht club for a weekend, call ahead on the VHF as soon as you're within range and reserve a slip. When you're safely tied up, you can explore the area on foot, on rental bicycles, or by dinghy.

TIPS FOR PLANNING A WEEK-LONG CRUISE

The only problem with a week's vacation on a boat is that the time goes too fast. To enjoy every moment, prepare yourself by making a cruise plan. Get everyone involved and plan destinations that include everyone's interests. If you're cruising with children, include visits to harbors with parks and museums (and an ice cream parlor!) or tourist towns with attractions to visit. If your kids don't travel well, don't plan a marathon of long days under way—plan short runs so you can stop and get off the boat and enjoy time ashore. Marinas and yacht clubs where there's a swimming pool are a popular draw for cruising families. So are those with a volleyball net and video arcade.

A cruise plan can be as simple as roughing out an itinerary of where you want to go and how long you want to stay there or as detailed as calculating mileage, speed, and fuel consumption for every leg of the trip. But a cruise plan should not be carved in stone. It's better to have alternate destinations so you can be flexible and ride out any changes in the weather. If you're new to boating, avoid long runs when you'll be at the helm all day. If you do plan a long day, make sure there's a safe harbor at a halfway point where you can stop if there's a threatening weather change.

As you cruise, you develop a cruising style—a comfortable living pattern that you follow when aboard. Some people like to wake up early and get under way with the sun just rising. Others like to sleep late and take off in midmorning. Develop your own cruising style and make your plans according to it.

The combination of your boat speed and your cruising style determines just how far you'll travel in a day, so take all these into consideration as you plan a week aboard.

Quality cruising is better than quantity cruising. It's better to choose a few destinations and enjoy them than to scurry from one place to another just to say you logged so many miles or visited so many harbors. What's the sense of visiting a charming harbor town or country club marina if you don't have time to enjoy it?

Don't box yourself in by making plans to rendezvous with friends at a distant location that can only be reached if you have ideal weather conditions. Allow for at least one "weather" day when wind or rain (or both) keep you in port. And make your last day's run back to home port a short one so you'll have plenty of time to unload the boat and head for shore, sort of slowly cycle back into the rigors of land life.

MAKING A FLOAT PLAN

A float plan helps locate you if you haven't returned when scheduled and in case someone needs to reach you while you're under way.

If you'll be on the water for any length of time, write down a float plan, which is a brief schedule of where you'll be cruising and when you expect to return. Give it to a reliable person ashore who can be depended on to notify the Coast Guard if you don't return on schedule. If your plans change while you're cruising and you'll be late returning, make sure to notify this person that you've deviated from the plan.

The plan should list the names of the people aboard and whether any of them have a medical problem, describe your boat and give registration numbers, and indicate the date when you expect to return. If you have reservations at a marina, include its name, location, and telephone number and when you'll be there.

GLOSSARY

AFT toward, near, or at the stern of the boat; also applies to wind blowing over the stern

AMIDSHIP the middle or center part of the boat

ANCHOR ON when a boat drops its anchor too close to another boat

ANCHOR RODE the length of line or chain that lies between the boat and its anchor

BIMINI a canvas top over the helm station of a powerboat or covering the cockpit of a sailboat

BOLLARD a heavy iron fitting on a commercial dock or in a lock where a boat's mooring line can be secured

BOW the most forward part of the boat

BOW LINES lines used for docking that are tied from the starboard and port sides of the bow

BREAKWATER a barrier or structure in a harbor that stops the impact of waves on the shoreline or creates an entrance to a channel

BULKHEAD a wall or partition in the cabin of a boat; also refers to a wall near a shoreline, often made of rocks or boulders, designed to hold back water

BURDENED VESSEL (or give-way vessel) the boat or ship responsible for altering course or giving way to another in a crossing or overtaking situation

CAST OFF to remove all lines to a dock or pier when a boat prepares to leave

CLEAT a fitting with two horns used for securing lines on a dock or on the deck of a boat or to control sheets and halyards on a sailboat

CROSSCURRENT condition of seas when the wind is blowing from the opposite direction from the tide or current

DAYMARK an unlighted marker on a piling in the water or on the shore, visible in daytime and good visibility; usually has two signs facing in opposite directions

DOWNWIND the direction toward which the wind is blowing

DRAGGING ANCHOR an anchor that is not holding because it has lost its grip on the bottom

FENDER a cushion of various sizes and shapes placed between the side of a boat and a dock or pier to prevent damage to the boat

FENDER BOARD 2 × 6 wooden plank approximately 3 feet long used in front of fenders so that the wood, not the fenders, rubs against a rough dock or lock wall

FINGER PIER a small platform built off a larger pier that provides access to boats in slips

GLOSSARY

FIX the position of a boat determined by two bearings taken simultaneously

FLAKED describes an anchor line arranged in an orderly manner so it won't tangle when let out

FLY BRIDGE an elevated steering station on a powerboat where the helmsman has an unobstructed view of the water and surroundings; a popular feature on fishing and cruising boats, also called the flying bridge

FORWARD toward the bow or front of a boat

GROUND TACKLE the rig used for anchoring a boat, including the anchor, line or chain, and shackles

HEADWAY the forward motion of a boat as it goes through the water

HEAVE TO to stop the forward motion of a boat

HELM the steering gear of any boat, i.e., the tiller or wheel

HELMSPERSON the man or woman steering a boat

KEDGE OFF to haul on a line attached to an anchor set in deep water to pull a grounded boat free of the bottom

LANYARD a short rope or cord used for holding or fastening something, e.g., a knife or whistle

LEEWARD toward the lee or the direction toward which the wind is blowing

LIFELINES plastic-coated wire ropes that enclose the deck by running around the sides of a boat, providing a safety net for crew members walking on deck; sometimes have a release mechanism near the cockpit so you can get aboard without having to step over them

LOOKOUT a passenger or crew member who keeps watch for other boaters, waterskiers, and other traffic

MOORING BUOY a permanent buoy attached to a sinker or anchor, where you can tie a boat instead of dropping an anchor

MOORING LINES the lines used to tie a boat to a dock or pier

OVERSTEER the common mistake of making sharp exaggerated turns when steering a boat, resulting in the boat traveling in an S pattern.

OVERTAKE to pass a boat by approaching from its stern

PAY OUT to let out more line gradually, as in letting out anchor line

PFD stands for "personal flotation device," which is anything that is buoyant, such as a cushion, life vest, or life preserver ring

PILING the vertical wooden or metal post supporting a dock or piers or set at the ends of a boat slip in the water

PILOTING the act of navigating while using reference points and water depth to determine a safe passage

PORT to the left side of a boat; also, an opening for light or ventilation

PRIVILEGED VESSEL (stand-on vessel) the boat or ship with the right-of-way when meeting another boat in a crossing or overtaking situation

PYROTECHNICS devices or materials that activate propellants, i.e., flares that ignite

SCOPE the ratio of anchor line to the depth of water, usually 7 feet of line for every foot of water

SLACK WATER in tidal waters, the time when there is little or no current

SLIP an individual berth for a boat at a dock, usually with a finger pier

SNUG UP A LINE to pull a line tighter and secure it on a cleat

SPAR a boom or mast used to support sails or flags

SPRING LINES lines used for docking a boat, led from the middle of both sides or either side of a boat

STARBOARD to the right side of a boat

STEERAGE the response of the rudder to the helm as a boat moves through the water

STERN the aft or rear part of a boat

STERN LINES lines used for docking that are tied from the port and starboard at the rear of the boat

STERNWAY the backward motion of a boat as it goes through the water

SUNSHADE a semipermanent or nonpermanent fabric covering attached over the cockpit of a boat to shield boaters from the sun

SWING KEEL a retractable keel that permits the boat to sail in shallow waters and be transported on a trailer

TIDES the vertical rise and fall of ocean waters caused by the gravitational pull of the moon and the sun

TILLER the arm or stick attached to the rudder post of a sailboat, used to steer the boat

UPWIND the direction from which the wind is blowing

V BERTH arrangement in the forward cabin of many sail and powerboats made of two berths that join together at the peak of the bow of the boat; often the two cushions for the berths have an additional wedge that fills in the crutch of the V, making it one large berth

WAKE the track of disturbed water left behind a moving boat

WIND SCOOP a fabric cylinder to attach over a hatch tied to rigging on a sailboat that collects the wind and directs it down the hatch for ventilation

INDEX

Page numbers in italics refer to illustrations.

accidents, 67
after spring lines, *12*, 13, 14, 16–19, 135
aids to navigation, 89, 92–95, *93*
American Water Ski Association, *43*
anchors, anchoring, 27–35, 77
   Bahamian moors, 33–34, *34*
   checking of, 31, *32*, 125
   choosing of, 27–29, *28*
   cleaning of, 35, 134
   CME requirements for, 76
   in crowded anchorage, 31
   on cruises, 125, 133–134
   currents and, 33–34, *34*
   Danforth, 27–28, *28*, 134
   dragging of, 32–33
   etiquette of, 33
   flaked, 31
   hand signals for, 31, *32*, 35
   holding power of, 27–29
   kedging off with, 78
   lines, 31, 32, *33*, 35, 95, 125
   at a mooring, 21–22, *21*
   mushroom, 27–28, *28*
   "on," 33
   overnight, 27, 28, 133–134
   plow, 27, *28*
   safe anchorages for, 29–31, *30*
   secondary, 29
   stowing of, 125, 134
   techniques for, 31–34, *32*
   testing bottom conditions for, 31
   in thunderstorms, 61
   water depth and, 30–31, *30, 33*, 133
   waves and, 29–30, 33–34, *33–34*
   weighing, 34–35, 134
   wind and, 29–30, 33–34, *33–34*,
      133
antenna systems, 112–113, 114
   GPS, *122*, 123
   multipurpose, 122
apparent wind, 51, 56

"baby on board" areas, 137
backfire flame control, 72
backstays, 47
Bahamian moors, 33–34, *34*
barbecue grills, marine, 127
barometric pressure, drops in, 58
battens, 49, 125
beam-reaching, 52, 55
beating, 52, 55
bib parts, 126
bicycles, folding, 132
biminis, 130, 137
binoculars, 100, 101, 128, 130
blower systems, 10, 71–72
boarding policies, 67
boat camping, 133
Boating Safety Hotline, 67
bollards, 24
booms, 47–48, 49, 54, 56–57
boom vang, 56
bottom conditions, 31, 91
bowline (knot), 62, *62*
bow lines, 12, 14–20, 24, 25, 135
bow to bow meetings, 81, *81*
broad-reaching, 50, 52, 55
buddy boats, 131
bug repellents, 130
buoys, 92–95
   can, 93–94, *93–94*
   horseshoe, 68
   mid-channel markers, 93–94, *94*
   as moorings, 21–22, *21*
   nun, 93–94, *93–94*
   in Uniform State Waterway Marking System, 95
   whistle, 58, 95
"burdened," 81
burgees, 138

call signs, 74
camping, boat, 133
canals, *see* locks
can buoys, 93–94, *93–94*
cars, trailers and, 36–41, *37–38*

centerboards, 53
certificate of number, 66
change of address, 66
channels, 83–84, 94
Channel 16, VHF, 114–115
children, 137, 138
cleats, 15, *16*
clews, 47, 48, 49
close-hauled, *50*, 52–54
close-reaching, 52, 55
clove hitch, 62–63, *63*
club burgees, 138
CMEs (Courtesy Marine Examinations), 76–77
coastal piloting, 96–110
coast charts, 87
Coast Guard, U.S., 67, 74, 89, 114–115, 139
Coast Guard Auxiliary, 76–77
Coast Guard Hotline, 76
Coast Guard Ventilation Standard, 72
Coast Pilot, 89
coaxial cables, 113
cold fronts, 58, *59*
collisions, 79, 80–85
compasses, 97–100
   adjusting, 98–100, *99*, 103, 105, *105*
   getting a fix with, 101, *101*, 104–106, *106*, 109, *109*
   hand bearing, 97, 101, 104–105, *105*
   plotting a course with, 103–110, *105, 107*
compass roses, 89, 91–92, *91*, 97, 103, 104, *105*
console mount VHF radios, 74, 112–113, *112, 114*
contour lines, 89, 118
cooking fuel, 76, 125
coolers, 128
Courtesy Marine Examinations (CMEs), 76–77
crankcases, 11
crossing at an angle, 70, 81–82, *82*
cruises, cruising, 124–139
   anchoring on, 133–134
   boat camping on, 133
   with buddy boats, 131
   children aboard, 137, 138
   creature comforts on, 128–129
   dinghies and, *124*, 134–135, 138

INDEX

cruises, cruising (*continued*)
  documenting of, 131
  eating during, 127–28
  first-aid kits for, 130
  flag etiquette and, 138
  flexibility on, 138–139
  float plans for, 139
  food storage on, 127–128
  foul-weather gear for, 126
  laundry chores during, 129
  locks for, 135–136
  nautical charts and, 131, 133
  outdoor living during, 130
  and overnight stays at marinas, 29, 132
  pets on, 136–137, *136*
  security on, 135–136
  ship's papers for, 126
  shoreside activities and, 131–132
  slip rentals and, 132, 138
  space management and, 129
  spare parts for, 125
  style of, 138
  supplies for, 130–131
  systems check for, 125
  water supply for, 128
  "weather" days on, 138–139
  weekend, 137–138
  week-long, 138–139
currents, 96
  anchoring and, 33–34, *34*
  departing and, 11, 12, 13
  grounding and, 78
  making headway against, 3
  mooring and, 16, 18–19, 20
  picking up a mooring and, 21
  and plotting a course, 107–110, *108–109*, 120–121
  reading ranges and, 93

Danforth anchors, 27–28, *28*, 134
daymarks, 92, 94, *94*, 98
dead ahead, 51
dead reckoning, 100–101, 103–110, 120–121
depth sounders, 110, 111, 117–119, *117–118*
deviation tables, 99–100, *99*, 103
dewatering devices, 76, 79
digital depth sounders, 118, *118*
dinghies, *124*, 134–135, 138
discharge restrictions, 74–76
distress calls, 115
distress signals, 10, 69–70, 77
dividers, 97, 101–102, *102*, 104
docks, docking, 14–26, 63–64
  backing away from, *12*, 13
  currents and, 11, 12, 13
  mooring lines and, 11–19, *15*
  mooring to, 17–19
  pulling away from, 10–13, *12–13*, 83
  slips vs., 19
  using spring lines at, 12–13, *12–13*
  wind and, 11, 12, 13
  see also moorings, mooring
documentation, 66–67, 74
dogs, 136–137, *136*
Douglas protractor, 97–98
dragging anchors, 32–33
drawbridges, 94

electrical systems, 77, 125
electronic navigation, 111–119
emergency situations, 77–79
ensigns, 138
Environmental Protection Agency (EPA), 76
Equipment Requirements, Federal, 67
Erie Canal, 24
etiquette, for flags, 138
excess weather helm, 56
exhaust blowers, 71–72
exhaust ducts, 71–72

falling off, 54
Federal Communications Commission, 74, 111
Federal Equipment Requirements, 67
fender boards, 23, *23*, 63, *63*
fenders, 13, 19, 20, 23, *23*, 25, *25*, 63, *63*, 125, 129, 135
figure 8, 15, *16*, 63, *63*

finger piers, 19–20
fire extinguishers, 10, 70–71, 77
fires, 77
first-aid kits, 130
fishfinders, 118–119, *119*
fishing markers, 95
fishing towers, 18
fishing vests, 68, *68*
fixes, 101, *101*, 104–106, *106*, 109, *109*, 120–121, 123
flags:
  distress, 69–70
  etiquette for, 138
flame arresters, 72
flares, 69–70
flasher-type depth sounders, 117–118, *117*
flemishing, 65, *65*
float coats, 68, *68*
float plans, 139
flotation aids, 68, *68*
fly bridges, 18
fog, 58, 70, 73, 96
folding bicycles, 132
food, for cruises, 127–128
foot, 47, 48
forecasts, weather, 11, 59–60, 77
forestays, 47, 49
forward spring lines, 12–13, *13*, 14, 16–19, *18*, 135
foul-weather gear, 126
fuel, fuel systems:
  CME requirements for, 76
  cooking, 76, 125
  fires and, 77
  reserve, 11
  taking on, 11, 125
  vapors, 10, 71–72, *72*
  ventilation for, 71–72, *72*, 76

gain, 113
gale warnings, 60
galley equipment, 76, 125
general charts, 87
getting under way, 10–13
"give-way vessels," 81
glossary, 141–143
going to starboard, 2–3
GPS (Global Positioning System), 110, 119, 120–123, *122*
gray water, 74
Great Lakes, 74, 75
grounding, 78–79
ground tackle, *see* anchors, anchoring

half hitches, 15, 63, *63*
halyards, 48, 49
hand bearing compasses, 97, 101, 104–105, *105*
handheld VHF radios, 74, 113–114, *114*, 125
hand signals, 21, 31, *32*, 35
  for waterskiing, 43–44, *43*
harbor charts, 87
hard-surface dinghies, 134–135
harnesses, safety, 137
hat clips, 137
hauling out, 40–41
heading up, 54
headway, making, 2–3
heating equipment, 76
heaving to, 67, 78
heeling, 6, 53, 57
helmsmanship, *see* navigation; steering
horseshoe buoy, 68
houseboats, *133*
hulls, 78–79
hurricane holes, 29
hybrid PFDs, 68, *68*
hypothermia, 68

ICW (Intracoastal Waterway), 95
Illinois River, 25
inboard boats:
  fire extinguisher requirements for, 70
  mooring of, 18
  single-screw, 9, 18
  before starting, 11
  stopping and backing of, 9
  ventilating engines of, 10
  see also powerboats

inflatable dinghies, *124*, 134–135
Inland Rules, 80–85
insects, 130
intake ducts, 71–72
International Rules, 80
intoxication, boating and, 67
Intracoastal Waterway (ICW), 95

jet-drive boats, 8, 9, 17
"jibe ho," 57
jib halyards, 49
jibing, 52, 56–57, *56*
"jibing," 57
jibs, 48–49, 52, 54, 55, 56–57
jib sheets, 49, 55, 125

kedging off, 78
kneeboards, 42–44
knot-meters, 97
knots, 62–65

ladders, swim, 129
launching, 39–40
laws and requirements, 66–79
  for backfire flame control, 72
  Courtesy Marine Examination (CME) for, 76–77
  enforcement of, 67
  equipment, 67
  for fire extinguishers, 70–71
  for navigation lights, 73
  PFDs and, 67–69
  for pollution, 74–76
  for ship station licenses, 74
  for sound-producing devices, 70
  for ventilation, 71–72
  for visual distress signals, 69–70
leaks, 79
left rudder, giving, 3
legends, 88–89, *88*
life jackets, offshore, 10, 68, *68*
lifelines, 63, *63*, 137
lift, 52–54, *53*, 55
lighted aids, 94
lighthouses, 92, 94
Light List, 94
lightning, 59–61
lights:
  distress, electric, 69–70
  as lock signals, 24
  navigation, 73, *73*, 125
  trailer, 37, 38, 39
line-of-sight signals, 111, 113
lines:
  anchor, 31, 32, *33*, 35, 95, 125
  bow, 12, 14–20, 24, 25, 135
  coiling, 11, 64, *64*
  flemishing, 65, *65*
  handling of, 64–65
  life, 63, *63*, 137
  for locks, 23–24
  mooring, 11–19, *15–16*, 40, 125
  paying out of, 22, 31
  securing of, to cleats, 15, *16*
  securing of, to moorings, 21–22
  spring, 12–13, *12–13*, 14–19, *18*, 135
  squeaky, 14
  stern, 12, 14–20, 24, 25, 135
  throwing of, 64, *64*
  tow, 8, 43, 44
locks (canals), 22–26
  boat handling on, 22–23
  locking through, 24–26, *25*
  preparation for, 23–24
  signals for, 24, 26
locks (security), 75–76, 135–136
Loran-C receivers, 110, 119, 120–123, *121*
lower shrouds, 48
luffing, 54, *55*
luffs, 48–49
lunch hooks, 29

magnetic bearing, 99–100, 103, *105*
magnetic north, *91*, 92, 97–98
main halyards, 49
mainsails, 48–49, 54, 56
main sheets, 47, 49, 55, 57

man overboard, 78
marine barbecue grills, 127
Marine Sanitation Devices (MSDs), 75–76
Marine Ship Service, 74
markers, 92–95
  for anchor lines, 31
  fishing, 95
  mid-channel, 93–94, 94
masthead lights, 73, 73
masts, 47–48
mid-channel markers, 93–94, 94
might makes right, 85
moorings, mooring:
  currents and, 16, 18–19, 20
  to a dock, 17–19
  leaving, 22
  lines, 11–19, 15–16, 40, 125
  in locks, 22–26
  picking up, 21–22, 21
  to a slip, 19–20, 20
  wind and, 16, 18–19, 20, 20
MSDs (Marine Sanitation Devices), 75–76
multifunction instruments, 117
mushroom anchors, 27–28, 28

national ensigns, 138
National Oceanic and Atmospheric Administration
    (NOAA), 60, 87, 89, 94
nautical charts, 30–31, 30, 87–110
  aids to navigation on, 89, 92–95, 93
  bottom conditions on, 91
  compass roses on, 89, 91–92, 91, 97, 103, 104, 105
  contour lines on, 89, 118
  cruising and, 131, 133
  legends on, 88–89, 88
  markers and buoys on, 92–95, 93–94
  measuring distance on, 101–102, 102, 103–110
  plotting a course on, 97–110
  publication date on, 89
  scale of, 88, 88, 101–102, 104
  soundings on, 88–89, 88, 90, 104, 110, 119
  tides on, 89, 90
navigation, 86–110
  aids to, 89, 92–95, 93
  basic tools of, 96–102
  for coastal piloting, 96–110
  compasses and, see compasses
  currents and, 107–110, 108–109, 120–121
  dead reckoning, 100–101, 103–110, 120–121
  depth sounders and, 117–119, 117–119
  electronic, 111–119
  fishfinders and, 118–119, 119
  GPS and, 110, 119, 120–123, 122
  lights, 73, 73, 125
  Loran-C receivers and, 110, 119, 120–123, 121
  multifunction instruments for, 117
  nautical charts and, see nautical charts
  plotting a course, 102–110
  speedometers and, 115–117, 116
  VHF radios and, 111–115
  working out fixes in, 101, 101, 104–106, 106, 109,
    109, 120–121, 123
near-shore buoyant vest, 68, 68
netting, safety, 137
NOAA (National Oceanic and Atmospheric
    Administration), 60, 87, 89, 94
No Discharge Zones, 75–76
nonpyrotechnic signals, 69–70
Notice to Mariners, 89
number, certificate of, 66
nun buoys, 93–94, 93–94

offshore life jackets, 68, 68
offshore winds, 18, 18
outboard boats:
  dinghies, 134–135
  in hauling out, 41
  locks for, 136
  mooring and, 17
  refueling of, 11
  shift and throttle controls on, 3–4
  steering of, 4–6, 5
  stopping and backing of, 9
  during thunderstorms, 61
  turning of, 8
  see also powerboats

outhauls, 48, 49
oversteering, 6, 7, 8
overtaking, 70, 82–83, 83, 85

parachute flares, 69–70
parallel rules, 97–98, 97, 103
PASS, 71
passing water, 7
personal flotation devices (PFDs), 11, 44, 77
  care and storage of, 69
  for children, 137
  man overboard and, 78
  types of, 67–68
pets, 136–137, 136
plow anchors, 27, 28
points of sail, 50, 51–52, 55
pollution, 74–76
polyvinyl chloride (PVC), 126
port, 2–3
portable toilets, 75–76
port-side landings, 17–18
port tack, 52, 57
powerboats:
  backing up of, 8–9
  bow to bow meetings of, 81, 81
  club burgees on, 138
  crossing at an angle, 81–82, 82
  danger zones of, 81
  inboard, see inboard boats
  outboard, see outboard boats
  reversing of, 3–4, 7–9, 8, 18, 19, 31–32
  right-of-way and, 85
  shift and throttle controls on, 3–4, 7–8, 17–18
  speed of, 3–4, 100–101
  steering of, 1, 4–6, 8–9
  stopping of, 8–9
  in thunderstorms, 61
  wakes of, 4, 7
"prepare to jibe," 57
"prepare to tack," 54
"privileged," 81
propellers:
  grounding and, 79
  right-handed, 9, 17, 18
  torque, 7
propulsion, alternate means of, 76, 77, 129
protractors, 97–98, 97, 103, 107
pump-out stations, 75
PVC (polyvinyl chloride), 126
pyrotechnic signals, 69–70

rafting up, 135
ranges, reading, 93, 98–100, 99
reaching, 50, 50, 55–56
"ready about," 54
reciprocal, 104, 105
Red, Right, Returning, 92
Reed's Nautical Almanac, 89
refrigeration systems, 125
registration, 66
reserve fuel, 11
reverse, shifting into, 3–4, 7–9, 8, 18, 19, 31–32
right-handed propellers, 9, 17
right-of-way, see rules of the road
right rudder, giving 3
roaches, 49
rudders, 3, 7–8
Rule of Twelfths, 90
rules, parallel, 97–98, 97, 103
rules of the road, 80–85
  bow to bow meetings, 81, 81
  crossing a channel, 83
  crossing at an angle, 70, 81–82, 82
  leaving the dock, 83
  might makes right, 85
  overtaking, 70, 82–83, 83, 85
  powerboats vs. sailboats, 85
  for sailboats, 84–85, 84
running, 50, 50, 52, 56–57
running rigging, 47, 48, 49

safety:
  anchorages and, 29–31, 30
  chains, for trailers, 37, 37
  check, 125
  in emergency situations, 77–79

equipment, location of, 10
harnesses, 137
Hotline, 67
jibing and, 57
laws and requirements for, 66–79
netting, 137
during thunderstorms, 61
for waterskiing, 44
sailboats, 1, 45
  aerodynamics of, 50–52, 50, 52–54
  basic parts of, 46, 47–49, 47
  care of, 48
  club burgees on, 138
  dinghies for, 135
  at the dock, 10
  falling off, 54
  head-on meetings of, 84–85, 84
  heeling of, 6, 53, 57
  launching of, from trailers, 40
  lift of, 52–54, 53, 55
  luffing of, 54, 55
  points of sail on, 50, 51–52, 55
  running rigging on, 47, 48, 49
  sails on, 48–50, 53, 125
  standing rigging on, 47–48
sailing, 45–57
  abeam, 51, 55
  beam-reaching, 52, 55
  beating, 52, 55
  broad-reaching, 50, 52, 55
  charts, 87
  close-hauled, 50, 52–54
  close-reaching, 52, 55
  dead ahead, 51
  downwind, 56–57, 61
  grounding, 78
  heading up, 54
  jibing, 52, 56–57, 56
  language of, 46–47
  mooring, 18
  reaching, 50, 50, 55–56
  right-of-way in, 84–85, 84
  running, 50, 50, 52, 56–57
  sitting position in, 6
  systems check for, 125
  tacking, 52, 54–55, 55, 56, 57
  in thunderstorms, 61
  towing, 38
  trimming, 49, 50, 52–54, 53, 55, 55, 56
sea boots, 126
secondary anchors, 29
screen kits, 130
security, 135–136
set, current, 107–110, 108–109, 120–121
shift controls, 3–4, 7–8, 17–18
ship's papers, 125
ship station licenses, 74
sidekick coolers, 128
sidelights, 73, 73
signals:
  hand, 21, 31, 32, 35, 43–44, 43
  line-of-sight, 111, 113
  for locks, 24, 26
  in narrow winding channels, 84
  in overtaking situations, 82–83, 83
  pyrotechnic, 69–70
  sound, 70
  storm, 60, 60
  VHF radio, 111
  visual distress, 69–70
  waterskiing, 43–44, 43
single-axle trailers, 37, 37
single-screw inboard boats, 9, 18
ski vests, 44
slips, 19–20
  rentals, 132, 138
sloop rigs, 47
small craft advisories, 60
social logs, 131
sound-emitting aids, 95
soundings, 88–89, 88, 90
sound-producing devices, 70
sound signals, 70
speed:
  driving, with trailer, 39
  fires and, 77

speed (continued)
  logs, 100–101, 115–117, *116*
  for mooring, 17, 18
  plotting, 100–101, 103–110, 115–117, *116*
  of powerboats, 3–4, 100–101
  steering and, 7, 8, 9, 17, 18
  for waterskiing, 44
  wind, 60, 61
speedometers, 115–117, *116*
spinnaker halyards, 49
spreaders, 47–48, 54
spring lines, 12–13, *12–13*, 14–19, *18*, 135
squall lines, 58
standing rigging, 47–48
"stand-on vessels," 81
starboard, 2–3
starboard-side approaches, 18
starboard tack, 52, 57
steering, 1–9
  basic terms for, 2–3
  with a compass, *see* navigation
  going straight and, 6–7
  lag time in, 6–7, 8
  mooring and, 17–19
  of outboard boats, 4–6, *5*
  over-, 6, 7, 8
  and pulling away from the dock, 12, *12*
  sailboats, *see* sailboats; sailing
  speed and, 7, 8, 9, 17, 18
  stopping and, 8–9
  with a tiller, 5–6, *5*
  towlines and, 8
  turning in, 7–8
  between two aids to navigation, 93
  wakes and, 7
  with a wheel, 4, *5*
stemlights, 73, *73*
stern-drive boats, 3–4, 8, 9, 11, 17, 40
stern lights, 12, 14–20, 24, 25, 135
sternway, 2–3, *2*
stopping, 8–9
storm signals, 60, *60*
storm warnings, 60
sunshades, 130, 137
surge brakes, 37
swim ladders, 129
systems checks, 125

tachometers, 100–101, 115
tacking, 52, 54–55, *55*, *56*, 57
telltales, *53*, 54, 56
throttle controls, 3–4
throwable devices, 68, *68*
thunderstorms, 58–61, 77
tides:
  anchoring and, 30–31
  on charts, 89, *90*

grounding and, 78
mooring and, 17
and plotting a course, 106–110
pulling away from dock and, 11, 12
Rule of Twelfths for, 91
tables, 89
tight maneuvering situations, turning in, 4, 7
tillers, 5–6, *5*, 57
toilets, 75–76, 125
torque, propeller, 7
tow bars, 8
towing, 8
  capacity, of cars, 37
  dinghies, 135
  in grounding situations, 79
towing services, 74, 79
towlines, 8, 43, 44
trailers, 36–41, *36*
  backing up of, 38–39, *38*
  basic rig for, 37, *37*
  braking with, 39
  checking of, 38
  driving with, 38–39
  hauling out and, 40–41
  launching from, 39–40
  safety chains for, 37, *37*
  sailboats and, 38, 40
  single-axle, 37, *37*
  weight capacity of, 37
transducers, underwater, 118
transmissions, 3–4, 8
trimming, 49, 50, 52–54, *53*, 55, *55*, 56
true north, 91–92, *91*, 97–98
true wind, 51, 52
turning, 4, 7–8
turning to port, 2–3, *2*
Twelfths, Rule of, 90

underwater transducers, 118
Uniform State Waterway Marking System, 95
upper shrouds, 48
U.S. Aids to Navigation, 92–95, *93*

vang, boom, 56
vapors, gasoline, 71–72, *72*
vector diagrams, 107–108
ventilation systems, 10, 71–72, *72*
vests:
  near-shore buoyant, 68, *68*
  ski, 44
VHF radios, 79, 111–115, 131, 132, 138
  antenna systems for, 112–113, 114, 122
  checking of, 125
  console mount, 74, 112–113, *112*, *114*
  distress calls on, 115
  forecasts on, 60
  handheld, 74, 113–114, *114*, 125

ship station licenses for, 74
talking on, 114–115

wakes, 4, 79
  steering and, 7
  and towing dinghies, 135
warm fronts, 58–59, *59*
water bottles, 128
water depth:
  anchorages and, 30–31, *30*, *33*, 133
  on charts, 88–89, *88*, *90*, 104, 110, 119
water skiing, 8, 42–44, *42*
  choosing waterskis for, 44
  hand signals for, 43–44, *43*
  PFDs for, 68
waves:
  anchorages and, 29–30, 33–34, *33–34*
  steering and, 6–7
  thunderstorms and, 61
  wind speed and, 61
way points, 120
weather:
  days, on cruises, 138–139
  fog, 58, 70, 73, 96
  forecasts, 11, 59–60, 77
  thunderstorms, 58–61, 77
weekend cruises, 137–138
week-long cruises, 138–139
Weems-Zweng protractors, 97–98
weighing anchor, 34–35
Western Rivers Systems, 95
wheel(s):
  blocks, 40, 41
  steering with, 4, *5*
whistle buoys, 58
wind:
  apparent, 51, 56
  cold fronts, 58
  departing and, 11, 12, 13
  fires and, 77
  grounding and, 78
  mooring and, 16, 18–19, 20, *20*
  offshore, 18, *18*
  picking up a mooring and, 21, *21*
  safe anchorages and, 29–30, 33–34, *33–34*, 133
  scoops, 130
  speed, 60, 61
  steering and, 6–7
  thunderstorms and, 59
  true, 51, 52
  warm fronts and, 58
  see also sailboats; sailing

yacht ensigns, 138